GENERATIONS LEARNING TOGETHER

LEARNING ACTIVITIES FOR INTERGENERATIONAL GROUPS IN THE CHURCH

Donald Griggs

Patricia Griggs

A Griggs Educational Resource

published by

Abingdon / Nashville

ISBN 0-687-14050-1

PREFACE

Greetings to our colleagues in church education:

This book has been a long time in the making. Pat and I/Don and I have been working at teaching persons of various ages together in one class for about ten years now. We have sensed a tremendous value to this style of teaching. We sense that many others in churches across the country have been discovering the values of involving mixed age groups in common learning experiences. If you share an interest in and commitment to planning for generations learning together then we welcome you to the adventure of exploring ways to approach this style of teaching.

Perhaps you too have searched for resources to guide you in planning for intergenerational learning activities and have been frustrated, as we have, in not being able to find much that was helpful. We have had to create from scratch, adapt from other resources, and experiment with resources and activities to see what would work. Sometimes we were successful and other times we had to start over again to see if there was another way to make it work.

Many persons have written and spoken to us about their experiences of teaching intergenerational groups. And, many have encouraged us to use our experiences and our publishing enterprise in order to pull together some resources that might be helpful to others who plan for generations learning together. So, we have taken the suggestions seriously and have responded to the encouragement to present in this book some basic principles,
    some planning suggestions,
        and some possible session plans.

From its beginnings Griggs Educational Service has been a family enterprise. We have three generations working together in various aspects of the enterprise. We can attest to the fact that there is a lot that is learned and a lot of growth happens as a result of our struggles together as parents, grandparents, children and grandchildren in a common life, work and ministry. Each generation has its own gifts, its own insights, its own needs. A family, a community, a church is not whole unless the gifts, insights, and needs of all its members are brought together in a shared life of love and commitment.

We three generations of Griggs persons wish for you the joy, excitement and sense of satisfaction that comes from having worked hard to produce a program that responds to the real needs and interests of persons in your church.

We like to get letters from others. Write to us if you have something to share related to your experiences in working with persons of many ages in your church. We would like to hear about ways this book has been helpful. Also, we would like to hear your own suggestions and ideas.

Livermore, California
June, 1976

Don and Pat Griggs
with Cathy, Scott, and Mark
and Ray and Rhoda Griggs

GENERATIONS LEARNING TOGETHER

Table of Contents

PART I:
SOME BASIC CONCERNS
PURPOSE OF THE BOOK

We have written this book for. . .

Church Educators who are seeking a resource to guide them, and those with whom they work, in thinking about and planning for intergenerational learning activities in their churches.

Leaders and Teachers of intergenerational programs who are seeking some specific guidelines, resources, and session plans to help them in their planning and leading.

Pastors and teachers in small churches where many of the activities in the church's regular program are already intergenerational. Hopefully, this book will serve as an additional resource in their planning.

Persons in larger churches who are seeking ways to develop some programs that bring persons of several generations closer together in the life of the church.

Denominational leaders of the churches of America who search for resources to recommend to churches and persons for whom they have some leadership responsibilities.

The Book includes **four** major parts. . . .

I. BASIC CONCERNS

In this section we attempt to highlight some of the practical administrative and planning concerns that face all who intend to work at developing a program for generations learning together.

Several of the articles in this section are of special importance to **administrative persons.**

- Start With A Task Group
- Try a Pilot Project
- Some Settings for Generations Learning Together
- A Training Event for Prospective Leaders

Other articles are intended primarily for those who will be **leaders** or **teachers** of intergenerational groups:

- Planning for Generations Learning Together
- Cues to Participation and Interaction
- Getting Started With a Group
- Roles of Leaders and Participants

The remaining articles will be of general interest to all who become involved in any way with the whole concept or practice of generations learning together.

II. FORMATION OF CHRISTIAN IDENTITY

This monograph is included to provide some theoretical reflection on a subject of great concern to all who preach, teach, and lead in the life and ministry of the church. In the space of eight pages we attempt to respond to the question, "How is a Christian identity formed?" Needless to say this is not the only, nor the best, answer to the question. But, it is one answer that may stimulate other questions and answers for those who read the monograph.

III. SESSION PLANS

This section on Session Plans is the "heart" of the book. However, if persons turn to this section first without looking at either of the first two sections they may miss the point. These session plans do not stand alone. They are presented within the framework of some very basic concerns about teaching and learning.

Even though the session plans are organized into nine units it is **not** intended that a planning committee would use them in the sequence in which they appear. It would be an unusual situation where **all** the session plans would **ever** be used.

It is our intention that planners and/or leaders select some of these units/sessions to use as the **starting point** for their planning. The session plans are all **samples** of what is possible. We would expect persons to be selective of what we have presented; to adapt, revise and rearrange what we have written so that it will "fit" the local situation.

IV. ADDITIONAL ACTIVITIES AND RESOURCES

In this small section persons will find a wealth of information. There are some other persons and places where resources and information are available to assist with designing teaching strategies for intergenerational groups. The resources have been checked for the availability and the persons have been contacted to be sure they are willing to respond if they hear from you. We have personal knowledge of each of these resources. Some of them we have incorporated into our own teaching, and we believe that we can recommend them all without any reservation.

We have thought that this book could be used in a variety of settings. . . .

. . . . As a **resource book** for a denominational or ecumenical training event for key persons who are seeking to develop skills and resourcefulness in the whole area of intergenerational learning activities.

. . . . As a **planning guide** for a local church committee or task group which is exploring the possibilities of implementing a program of generations learning together in their own church.

. . . . As a **curriculum resource** for leaders and teachers who have responsibilities for leading a group of families or persons from two or more generations in a common learning experience.

SOME PERSONAL EXPERIENCES

When one attempts to summarize and share personal experiences in a printed form such as this, it becomes very obvious that much is lost in the process. Pat and I/Don and I have been thinking about and working with intergenerational groups in the church for more than ten years. We have experimented with various sizes and structures of groups. We have tried a wide variety of teaching activities and resources. And, mostly we have felt very good about our experiences of relating to and leading groups across the ages. We want very much to share with you some of what we have learned, some of our enthusiasm, and some of our concerns. But, we find it difficult to capture in the written word all that seems important to share. Perhaps the best we can do is raise a few questions, offer some suggestions, outline some activities, point to some directions and then trust that you and others in your church will grow together in your own understanding and enthusiasm for generations learning together.

Our first experience of teaching children and parents in one class occurred about ten years ago in the Presbyterian Church in Livermore. With the help of a few persons and the cooperation of fifteen families we engaged in an experimental program which we called THE JUNIOR EXPERI-MENT. This program was described in an article in the March 1969 issue of COLLOQUY magazine. The article is reprinted beginning on page 5. After two years of experimenting with that program we were convinced that there was great potential for generations learning together. However, Don became involved in a specialized work of teacher education so that working directly with families and other intergenerational groups in a local church on a regular basis became more difficult.

Every opportunity that came along we tried to find ways to involve persons across the ages. In a one week summer conference for church teachers we met each day for one and a half hours with junior age children **and** teachers. They became one class, working together as fellow learners. Then for another ninety minutes we met only with the teachers to focus on concepts, skills, resources, and relationships that are basic to teaching in the church. This proved to be an effective way to do teacher training. Teachers were able to experience directly some of what their students experience and to identify in a more personal way with the situation of the learners.

For six weeks, before and during Advent, Pat led a program that was prepared for families and others of all ages to participate in a series of learning and creating activities. More than one hundred persons participated weekly in these forty-five minute sessions. With clear directions, interesting activities, concerns for all ages and a lot of helpers, persons of all ages became involved together in sharing their feelings and ideas about Advent and Christmas. Many, many persons asked, "When can we do something like that again?" The outline of this series is in our book TEACHING AND CELEBRATING ADVENT.

In a Family Bible Study Retreat that Don led for a neighboring church we discovered that all members of a family, and the church family, cannot only learn a lot when they do it together, but they can have a good time doing it. The basic outline of the activities included in that Retreat is presented in Unit One beginning on page 43.

A similar experience only on a much larger scale was when Don and Pat served as part of the leadership team for Family Festival 1972 sponsored by the Reformed Church in America. Here also, groups of families were to participate in Bible study together. The outline of the three sessions of Bible study for this occasion are presented in Unit Four beginning on page 77. In both the Retreat and the Festival setting we found that persons were able to participate and learn together despite the diversity of ages, interests and backgrounds.

Most recently Don has been conducting workshops in various parts of the country on the subject of "Planning for Intergenerational Learning Experiences." In each instance persons come to the workshop with little experience, but much motivation in this approach to teaching and learning. As a part of each workshop there is a one hour period where about a dozen children and youth join us to participate with ten to twelve adults from the workshop in a sample study session. Each time Don leads such a group of 20-25 strangers he wonders if it is going to work - and it does. Persons who participate in the sample session as well as those who observe are always impressed with how quickly the group becomes a group and how much they enjoy their experiences together. (An outline and description of this workshop are presented on pages 32-35.)

Many of the other session outlines come from Pat's teaching in our local church in Livermore with a team of experienced teachers. This class is offered in addition to Sunday School and is called the Celebration Hour. Here children beginning at first grade and going through sixth grade meet each Sunday with Junior High and Senior High student "helpers" and a variety of adults in a continually changing program of exploration and study. Units of study are offered in 4 to 8 week series. This allows for a variety of teaching styles and methods to be used, a continually changing staff, and a number of units of subject matter to be covered. While the program is offered primarily for the children in grades one to six, it is obvious that the number of Junior and Senior High students and the number of adults that are involved in the class make it an intergenerational learning unit. While there may be one or two adults in the class who have done the planning, there may be as many as 15 other persons who have not been involved in the planning but are there learning and growing with the younger students.

THE JUNIOR EXPERIMENT*

It is five minutes before ten o'clock on Sunday morning, the opening day of church school in September. I look around the room. Everything is ready. The tables are set for painting. There are plenty of old shirts. The phonograph is set. I'm nervous, but I guess I am ready.

Five minutes from now, thirty people will be coming from the worship service and all of them, including the parents will paint. I warned them that this would be an experimental class. But I didn't tell them they'd have to paint the first day!

The first few minutes are a little tense. There are big fathers, dressed-up mothers, and bright-eyed kids. Everyone puts on paint shirts amidst nervous laughter and cautious conversation. The fathers, buttoned into paint shirts, wish there were an escape hatch handy, wondering how they got conned into this. But they are good sports. Everyone responds to my instructions:

> "We are going to spend an hour a week together this school year learning and growing together. We are going to work hard at sharing our ideas, feelings, and questions with one another. There are many ways to communicate. Mostly we use words. But words are often confusing, especially when adults use big words that children cannot understand. So I want you to use the materials on the tables to express your feelings and experiences related to the previous hour of worship. We are not interested in pretty pictures. We are only interested in your own expression through paint of what the worship meant to you. Any questions? Everyone paint."

They start cautiously. Parents feel strange because they haven't done anything like this for years. Children feel a little intimidated because of the adults. One by one, people begin. As each painting is finished, it is displayed on the wall. Some do a second and third painting. Everyone participates and has fun. One father says, "That was a great experience!" A child comments, "The parents' paintings aren't any better than ours!"

Thus, the Junior Experiment was launched in the First Presbyterian Church of Livermore in the fall of 1967.

As Associate Pastor, I was responsible for the church's educational program for children through the eighth grade. I had often dreamed of including parents and children in one class. After several months of planning and consulting with the children's department, we decided to give it a try.

Livermore is a unique city because many people in the community are scientists, physicists, chemists, engineers, and skilled craftsmen employed by the Lawrence Radiation Laboratory, a facility of the Atomic Energy Commission. Experiments, innovations, dreams of doing a job better are a part of the community's climate.

DETERMINING OBJECTIVES

Our primary objective in the Junior Experiment was to increase communication between parents and children. Fifth and sixth graders are perfect. They have wide interests, are able to express themselves, and understand adults pretty well. And they haven't yet reached adolescence, when they want little to do with their parents.

A second objective was to include the children as a responsible part of the worshiping, studying, serving community of the church. Too often, church programs segregate and isolate the generations, contributing more to the gap. Also, the image of the church school is as a child-care center, while adults do the serious business of being the church. No wonder children don't feel they belong.

Another objective was to place church education in the context of the family's life in church and home. We live in a time when specialists in every phase of education, recreation, and church life threaten to take the parents' role of nurturing their children. There is evidence that adults **and** children can be more motivated in church education when they participate together to their mutual benefit.

Our fourth objective was to provide opportunities for children and parents to satisfy their natural curiosity and desire to learn by teaching inductively. We were convinced that the only worthwhile learning would be a result of a person's exploration of ideas, exposure to various media, and discovery of those things which give meaning to his own life.

DESIGNING THE PROGRAM

There were three major parts of our program:

*Class for Parents **and** Children.* This happened on Sunday morning with one hour of worship and forty-five minutes of study during the regular adult education period between services. I taught this class, using a variety of resources. There were also several field trips, a swim picnic, and a potluck supper. On these occasions, the other members of the family were also included.

Class for Children. On Wednesdays from 3:45 to 5:15 the children met for study. The period began with games, singing, and refreshments, with an hour and a quarter of study. Two teachers were responsible for this class.

A different parent brought refreshments each week and participated as an observer. The class used the United Church Curriculum adapted to the particular situation.

Class for Parents. Once a month I met with parents to discuss the same materials the children studied on Wednesdays.

A tuition fee of $20.00 was charged each family for the year. This money provided additional resources for each child, child care for teachers' children, expenses for field trips, a picnic, potluck supper, and curriculum.

The most ambitious objectives can look great on paper. But unless they capture the enthusiasm of the participants, you have achieved nothing. That is why planning for the first session was so important. There was a reason for starting with creative painting. Whatever we did the first session had to motivate adults and children. Anything verbal probably would have reached only one of the groups. There also had to be participation, involvement, and self-expression in order for everyone to feel committed to the class. What better media than paint? And it proved to be the perfect icebreaker. When all the paintings were posted, you could not tell which were done by adults and which by children - a great equalizing factor. At the second session, each person shared with the whole class what his painting meant to him. There were not judgments of paintings, only appreciation for what each painting expressed.

The unit theme for the next ten weeks was worship. Since children worshiped weekly with their parents, they wanted to understand the meaning of what they did. We suspected the parents had something to learn too.

WHY DO WE WORSHIP THE WAY WE DO?

We decided there must be a way for people to recognize the reason for the order of worship. We followed these steps:

> The teacher asked: "What are some things people do that require a certain order or form?

> The class responded: "Write a letter." "Build a model airplane." "Bake a cake." "Cut out and sew a dress."

> The teacher inquired: "What would happen if we signed our name on the letter before we wrote 'Dear....' or if we did not follow the directions, recipe, or pattern?"

The class responded: "It wouldn't look right. It would not come out right."

The teacher agreed and summarized, saying: "There is a way to bake a cake or build a model. And you are right. If we don't follow the directions, we will get confused and it won't come out right. Have any of you ever wondered about the way we do things in our worship service?

Time was allowed for comments and questions. Then the teacher and his wife did a role-play to illustrate the meaning of the order of worship. The teacher presented a beautifully wrapped package to his wife. She responded, "What is this for? It is not my birthday. How come a gift?"

The teacher said, "I love you and want you to have this gift. Open it."

"It is a watch. It is beautiful! You shouldn't have done it! What did I do to deserve such a gift? I don't have anything for you. I'm so happy, but I'm sorry I don't have something to give you."

"Your happiness is enough. I knew you needed a watch, and I wanted you to have one."

Then the man and woman talked a few minutes, remembering the first watches they got as kids, how they felt so grown up, how important watches are, and how valuable time is.

The wife concluded by saying, "I'm so happy, I am going to bake you a cherry pie." She kissed him and the role-play was over.

The teacher then gave each person a copy of a bulletin with the order of worship, divided the class into six small groups, and asked them to discuss the question, "What is the connection between the role-play you just saw and the order of worship we follow in church?"

After a few minutes of discussion, they said:

"God gives us Jesus because he loves us."
"We show we are happy with praises and thanksgiving because of God's gift."
"Remembering the first watches is like remembering Jesus and the disciples in the scripture and sermon."
"What is the point of the cherry pie?"
"That is like our gifts to God in comparison to his gift to us."
"I see. You really can not give your offering to God until you have heard and accepted God's gift yourself."

Almost everyone in the class had some reason for why we worship the way we do.

HOW DO YOU WRITE SERMONS?

We invited our minister to class to talk about the many ways he finds ideas for sermons. He also told the class what his topic was for the next Sunday. The class was divided into small groups to think of some questions for him. The minister said he would think about the questions as he prepared his sermon.

The next Sunday, parents and children received a copy of the questions they had asked the previous week. They were asked to write any notes they wanted during the sermon and be prepared to discuss the sermon in class.

Adults and children listened as they never had before. Almost everyone had a page of notes. And they could hardly wait to get to class and discuss them.

PARTICIPATING IN WORSHIP

One of the children asked, "Can we help in the service?"

We involved families in many ways. We asked them to serve as greeters for several weeks. We spent one Sunday coaching children to be ushers, and they did an excellent job for a month. One Sunday in class, everyone wrote prayers of confession and thanksgiving and calls to worship. Several prayers were selected and used in the Order of Worship. A prayer of confession, written by a fifth grader follows:

> "O God, forgive us for living in a nutshell, trying to improve our own lives, while other persons are in great need. Forgive us for working too hard to polish ourselves while forgetting what Jesus taught us. Forgive us for wandering from you and your teachings, for traveling alone, for forgetting that you are with us. Hear our prayers in Jesus' name.
>
> Amen."

PARENT-CHILD CONVERSATION

On several occasions, pairs of chairs were placed together in the classroom to allow for conversations between a parent and his child. Prior to Christmas, we followed this procedure:

1. The class was told that for five to ten minutes the parent was to share with the child some of his childhood memories of Christmas. The kids really enjoyed this. Most of them learned something about their parents they had not known.

2. The children were asked to share with the parents what they liked most about Christmas. This gave the parents insight into the children's joys and expectations.

3. Each pair was instructed to choose one favorite family tradition to share with the rest of the class.

4. We spent the last twenty minutes of class sharing these traditions. This sharing provided ideas for other families to consider.

THE BIBLE: THE BOOK OF THE CHURCH

After Christmas, the unit of study for the next several months was the Bible. The first Sunday we showed the filmstrip WRITE IT IN A BOOK (Produced by The Graded Press). Also, the book KNOW YOUR BIBLE by Mary Alice Jones was given to each family. The whole class was asked to list their questions about the Bible so that we could plan the lessons to answer them. Some of the questions were:

> "Did God write the Bible?"
> "Is the creation story true?"
> "If some of the things in the Bible didn't really happen, why should we believe the Bible?"
> "How did the Bible get started?"
> "How long did it take to write the Bible?"
> "Did the people who wrote the Bible know they were writing scripture?"
> "Will there ever be any additions to our Bible?"
> "How could Abraham have lived six hundred years?"
> "What is the difference between the King James and the Revised Standard Version of the Bible?"

We felt the main idea to get across was that the Bible is the result of the work of many authors. Even on a subject like creation, there are two stories which contradict each other or at least provide different perspectives. If the class could see this, perhaps they could accept the fact that the Bible is very much the words of men as well as the word of God. To achieve this goal, we planned two basic learning experiences.

The class was divided into two groups, each with adults and children. Each person was given a mimeographed worksheet, divided into three columns, with these questions in the middle column:

> "How long did creation take?"
> "Where did creation take place?"
> "When in the process was man created?"
> "When in the process was woman created?"
> "From what substance were man and woman created?"
> "What is the relationship between male and female?"
> "What is the relationship between man and God?"

Heading the first column was Genesis 1:1-2:4 and heading the third column was Genesis 2:5-24.

A space was provided for answers. One group was assigned each of the passages from Genesis. Each group was responsible for answering the same questions based on the content of their passage. Each group had fifteen minutes to read its passage and answer the questions.

Their answers were not only different but sometimes contradictory. After all the questions were answered, the teacher asked, "Based on the little you know about the beginnings of the Bible and using common sense, how do you account for these differences?" A fifth-grade boy responded, "That is easy! Two different guys wrote two different stories and somebody else put them together later."

The point became clear to the whole class. Of the thirty people in the class, only four or five had known there were two accounts of creation and that there was more than one source of the scriptures. They all had now experienced both stories.

At the beginning of the next class, the teacher asked for several volunteers to dramatize the point of the previous week's lesson.

A father and his two sons volunteered to be the "model" family. Their only instructions were that they would be brought into the room one at a time and interviewed by the teacher about the younger son's birth.

A woman volunteered to be the recorder. She would record the responses of each family member. Then, after all had responded, she was to present to the class a narrative of the younger child's birth.

The father and older son were dismissed from the room. The younger son was asked questions about the time of day he was born, his father's reactions, his brother's reactions, how his name was chosen. His answers were based on stories he had heard in the family. Then, in turn, the older son and father were asked the same questions. As expected, the answers differed.

Our recorder then gave her account of the younger son's birth. Naturally, she selected some "facts" and left out others. She presented her understanding of the event in a narrative which included some aspects of each person's story. Also, because she felt the mother's perspective was missing, she made up some material to fill in that gap.

The class became excited. They were quick to see the connection between this demonstration and last week's discussion.

Again, the inductive, or discovery, approach to learning worked. Parents **and** children learned. Parents **and** children were more excited about learning. Parents **and** children enjoyed learning **together**.

Many of our objectives were fulfilled. However, we faced some obstacles:

1. There are no curriculum materials produced for this kind of class. It requires imaginative and innovative teachers.

2. A class of thirty is the maximum size. But most congregations have more than fifteen families. How can we plan to involve more families? Can we justify the time and energy spent on so few?

3. Many teachers, pastors, or laymen would not feel comfortable teaching adults and children in the same class.

4. There were many times when adults talked over kids' heads. The best remedy is for the teacher to say, "Johnny, did you understand what Mr. Jones just said?" "Mr. Jones, would you please repeat what you said so Johnny can understand you?"

At the end of the year, a child said, "I learned as much about Daddy as I did about the Bible." A mother whose son and husband attended the class said, "I could hardly wait to find out what happened in Junior Experiment each Sunday. The whole family benefited from it."

Where do we go from here?

We need versatile, helpful curriculum materials to use in such classes. We need to try many experiments to discover new teaching approaches in the church. We know the family can learn and grow together; we need to provide more opportunities for it to happen.

START WITH A TASK GROUP

Most churches have a committee responsible for the Christian Education program in that church. Committees often have more concerns and responsibilities than can be handled in the time available for their meetings. In order to facilitate the consideration of and planning for a program of intergenerational learning it is important to recruit a special task group to do the work.

Task group membership could include:

- Representatives from C. E. Committee
- A staff person
- An experienced teacher or two
- A couple of parents and grandparents
- Two or three young persons.

The task group may take steps such as the following:

1. **Read** this book plus several of the resources listed in "Part Four: Additional Activities and Resources".

2. **Observe** a program in another church in town or nearby where persons of many ages are involved in the same group.

3. **Evaluate** the church's present program in order to identify all the times and places where persons of various ages are already involved or where they could become involved.

4. **Interview** persons across age groups in the church to determine some of the interests and needs that are present among members of the church that might be responded to with a program of intergenerational learning.

5. **Determine** whether or not a program to involve generations learning together is needed or has the possibility of success in the church.

6. **Establish** some basic goals for whatever program may be developed in the church.

7. **Design** a program, perhaps a pilot project, for generations to learn together. Decide which age groups will be involved: children and adults, whole families, mixed age groups from various families, or other combinations of ages.

8. **Identify** the particular skills and traits that are necessary for persons who are going to serve as leaders of intergenerational groups.

9. **Recruit** persons to be the leaders of whatever programs or groups are designed. It is best if two persons share leadership of a group of up to twenty-five persons. If there are more than twenty-five persons then it may be wise to organize two groups each with two leaders.

10. **Publicize** and promote the program within the whole congregation. Be sure to interpret the unique goals and features of this program so that persons are clear as to why they are saying "yes" or "no".

11. **Provide** opportunities and/or funding for the leaders to receive additional training and enrichment to help equip them for their leadership responsibilities.

12. **Continue** to support and encourage the leaders and participants in the program. Stay in touch with the program in order to help with the evaluation after the program has been completed.

The steps in this process would be appropriate for a task group on any new program, not just intergenerational. Our intent is not to suggest that a church's whole program become intergenerational, but to suggest some procedures and resources that may contribute to planning for new activities as part of the total church program.

TRY A PILOT PROJECT

Instead of launching a new program for the whole congregation it may be wiser to start small, with a pilot project. There is a significant advantage to planning for a smaller group, or a shorter time-frame, in order to test the feasibility of intergenerational activities. It is easier to change, adjust, experiment with, relate to and evaluate a small program. After working through the whole process with a pilot project it will be easier to anticipate how a larger group will respond and participate. It may be that the original task group would be responsible for the pilot project so that they will know better whether or not to continue their planning to involve a larger portion of the congregation. One possible way to implement the pilot project is outlined below. **The pilot project would occur after a task group had accomplished some of the tasks outlined in the previous section.**

STEP ONE: Invite persons to participate

In order to have a group to work with there are several ways persons could be recruited to participate in the group. A group of between 20 and 30 persons would be best.

a. A couples group or other organization in the church could agree that such a project is something they want to participate in as a major part of their group's program. They could either volunteer their group to be the planners or leaders or their families could become the participants.

b. An announcement of the pilot project with an invitation to participate could be published in the church's newsletter or Sunday bulletin. Be sure to specify the range of ages and whether or not partial families and singles are included.

c. A representative sample of the members of the church could be selected as potential participants. They could all receive a phone call or letter of invitation to participate. Be sure to include a diversity of ages, family status, and backgrounds.

STEP TWO: An Orientation Session

All persons who respond to the invitation to participate will attend an orientation session. The **purpose** of this session is to explain the reasons for the program and to outline what persons can expect to experience in the program. **All** persons who are expected to participate should be invited to the orientation session.

A possible **agenda** for the orientation session could be:

- A potluck meal
- A game or other process that helps persons become acquainted with each other.
- Singing a song or more
- Someone from the Task Group outlines the goals and plans for the program.
- Participants are encouraged to ask questions
- Leaders of the pilot project are introduced
- Spend 45-60 minutes to experience some sample activities that represent what persons can expect to experience in other sessions.
- Provide an opportunity for persons to indicate whether or not they plan to continue.
- Closing prayer, litany, or song.

STEP THREE: Three to Six Sessions

Select from this book, another source, or create your own plans for three to six sessions that will involve between 20 and 30 persons of various ages.

The leaders of the three to six sessions should consider seriously the suggestions presented in several other sections of this book. Look at "Planning for Intergenerational Activities", "Cues to Participation and Interaction," and "Getting Started with a Group."

STEP FOUR: Revise, Adjust, and Adapt

This is a pilot project. One of the features of a pilot project (the participants should be aware of this also) is that it is experimental which means that in the midst of the experiment it is possible to revise the plans, adjust the time schedule or adapt to the needs and interest of the participants. It is important for the task group persons and the leaders of the program to stay in communication with each other and with the participants. The participants will be able to offer a lot of feedback regarding the strong and weak points of the program based on their own experiences.

STEP FIVE: Evaluation

If the pilot project is intended to precede a larger, more extensive program then it is very important to evaluate the program cheerfully. Some possibilities to consider in the evaluation process are:

- Recruit someone at the beginning of the project who will guide the evaluation. This could be a member of the task group.

- Prepare a questionnaire that all participants, leaders and observers would complete. Keep the questionnaire as simple as possible. Include objective, data-type questions and also some open-ended, subjective questions.

- Conduct interviews with all, or some, of the participants.

- Through the questionnaire or interview the evaluator should focus on:

    a. General feelings, impressions of total program
    b. Number of sessions, length of sessions, time of sessions.
    c. Subject matter.
    d. Types of activities and resources
    e. Values of learning with persons of many ages.

- It is important to receive impressions and reflections on the experience from **all** ages of persons. Children, youth, adults, older adults will all have different perspectives to bring to the evaluation.

SOME SETTINGS FOR GENERATIONS LEARNING TOGETHER

Whether you are planning to conduct a pilot project or you intend to have a more extensive program of intergenerational learning there are a variety of settings that could be considered. The concept and practice of intergenerational learning can be implemented in many different settings. It would be necessary to consider the unique features, needs, and possibilities of each setting and to plan accordingly. Generations can learn together in many different times and places.

Sunday Morning Church School

- In small churches the total church education program could be intergenerational for all or part of the year.

- Where church school enrollment is limited to just a few persons in each grade level in children's and youth area it would be possible to involve all ages in one or two classes.

- In larger churches a special class could be formed for children of one age group with their parents **or** for a group of families.

- Another possibility is to combine one adult class with one children's çlass for a period of three to six weeks.

Family Nights

- Many churches have the custom of monthly family night programs. Our observation of many of these programs is that the families share a meal together then the children go one direction for their program, the youth another direction, and the adults do "their thing".

- It seems to us that the Family Night Program provides a natural setting to try one or more intergenerational learning activities.

- After a meal all the families could remain together, or families could be divided into smaller groups, in order to work together in the planned activities.

Vacation Church School

- Some churches have had success offering Vacation Church School as an evening program. It could be one or two weeks, four or five nights each week from 6:30 to 8:30 pm.

- Or, one night per week through the summer could be planned as Vacation Church School.

- The whole school could be planned for intergenerational groups or one class could be designated as an intergenerational class.

Retreats

- We have found the retreat setting to be a good way to introduce persons to intergenerational learning activities.

- The retreat could be at a conference center, at a church in another town, or at your own church.

- The retreat setting provides opportunities for sharing many different activities such as recreation, meals, worship, conversation, and study.

- As short as an overnight or as long as a week could provide good time for learning together in a retreat setting.

Short-Term Contracts

- A group of families could contract together where they would agree to meet for a set number of weeks, a specific time for each week, to focus on particular themes or subjects. Part of their contract would include responsibilities of individuals and families and ground rules for participation in the group.

- The Family Cluster Program emphasizes the importance of the whole cluster forming and agreeing to a contract. The contract can be open ended so that it can be revised at any time with the group's approval.

Days and Seasons of the Church Year

- Advent, Christmas, Easter, Pentecost and other special days and seasons provide an appropriate occasion for generations to be together for learning, celebrating, and sharing activities.

- On a special Sunday, or other day, it would be possible to have an extended period combining study, worship and fellowship where all ages participate in the same program.

PLANNING FOR GENERATIONS LEARNING TOGETHER

Planning for teaching, no matter what the subject or the age group, has some very basic principles and procedures that should be followed. Don has written two helpful resources that persons can use when planning for teaching in the church.

TEACHING TEACHERS TO TEACH

The first eight chapters deal directly with most of the factors that are involved in planning for teaching.

THE PLANNING GAME*

This is a simulation game that employs a manual and packs of 80 cards which teachers can use in small groups to help them work through the whole planning process.

What follows is a summary of some of the material which is included in our other two books on planning for teaching.

A *FIRST STEP* in the planning process is to respond to the question, "What am I going to teach?" To answer that question means that we focus on the **key concepts** and **main ideas** that will become the basis for the teaching session.

- It is better to focus on fewer concepts than to try to "cover" too many. One meaning of "to cover" is "to hide from view, to cover up." That is exactly what happens if we present too many concepts in one session. We cover up a lot of it and thereby hide it from view.

- We do not have to cover everything we know on the subject or everything that is in the lesson plan. Our primary responsibility is to **uncover** what is most important or appropriate for a particular session.

  Be selective.

  Work at uncovering key concepts.

  Don't worry about what has not been uncovered. There will be other sessions, other experiences for more uncovering.

- It is better to focus on concepts that are more concrete rather than those that are abstract. A concrete concept is something I can identify with personally as a result of my experience. Concrete concepts are based on life experiences. Abstract concepts are more vague, symbols that represent experiences in a more general way. Persons of all ages are helped more through starting with concrete concepts. Especially in intergenerational groups it is essential that the concepts presented be related to the life experiences of all the persons.

Keep the concepts simple, concrete, life-centered. Don't become simplistic, just simple. There is a good song with the words, "Tis a gift to be simple, tis a gift to be free." Perhaps that can be our theme song.

- It is better to keep concepts together that belong together. Students of all ages are helped more when concepts and main ideas are clustered around one theme, one event, one person, one experience than when concepts are presented in a random haphazard manner.

- It is better to develop concepts in a logical, sequential, step by step process than it is to present concepts in a random way.

* Send for catalog from Griggs Educational Service, 1731 Barcelona Street, Livermore CA 94550. The catalog includes descriptions of this book.

- Concepts can be introduced and developed in a variety of ways; through any of the following. . . .

   . . . .a story
   . . . .a question
   . . . .a definition
   . . . .a personal experience
   . . . .a saying or quotation
   . . . .a verse or passage of scripture
   . . . .a picture or other visual expression
   . . . .a report of an event
   . . . .a biographical account of some person

- Teachers need to be open to a wide variety of expressions by participants as they share what they think, believe, feel and value. Remember, concepts are formed by our experiences and everyone has a specific set of unique experiences. We are not seeking for unanimity of thought, rather we are accepting of a diversity of expression.

A *SECOND STEP* in the planning process is to respond to another question, "What will the participants experience and learn?" To answer that question means that the leader-teacher will be making some determination of the **objectives** for the particular session. To set some specific objectives means that the leader intends for something to happen to the persons who participate, they will be different, think different, or act different to some degree at the end of the session than they did at the beginning. (Notice that in each of the units and sessions in **Part Three - Session Plans** there is stated a specific set of objectives.)

- **Objectives** are more specific than **goals.**

- **Goals** are large enough to spend a life-time pursuing. Goals give us general direction for our teaching and learning. Goals are often beyond our reach. Goals are too general to use for planning and evaluating specific teaching sessions.

  Example of a **goal**: "Persons will become more loving and caring toward other persons."

- **Objectives** are more specific, tangible, achievable. Objectives are written in terms of what students can be expected to accomplish in particular learning activities. Objectives are little steps in the direction of a larger goal. Objectives are helpful guidelines for teachers in their planning and evaluating of teaching activities.

  Example of an **objective**: "At the end of the period of study the participants will be able to visit a lonely, elderly person to share a simple gift and conversation with that person."

A *THIRD STEP* is to respond to the question "What are we going to **do** to uncover the main ideas and to achieve the objectives?"

Once the **key concepts** are focused and the **instructional objectives** determined, the teacher should have a clear sense of direction. The next step in planning is to design the **teaching activities** that will most effectively communicate the concepts and achieve the objectives. The accent is upon **activity**.

Often the teacher begins preparation by asking, "What am I going to say to the class about the concept of 'covenant'?" That is the wrong question because answering it leads the teacher to think about what the teacher is going to **tell** the students. A more appropriate question would be "What are the students and I going **to do** about the concept of 'covenant'?"

Answering this question leads directly to thinking about activities, what persons will be doing in the classroom to learn.

17

Teaching activities are defined as all those actions of students and teachers in the classroom. There are many dozens of possible teaching activities that can be organized into several categories as illustrated by the diagram below.

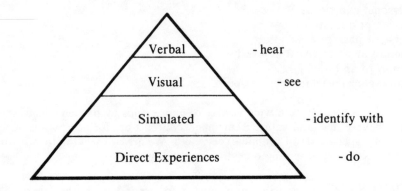

Verbal Activities have been the most common means used in teaching. Teaching activities in this category are: lecture, discussion, recording, sermon, story, reading, and any other type of verbal presentation that depends primarily upon the hearing of the learner. The evidence is that most people do not learn well just by hearing something. In order to be effective, verbal activities must be accompanied by other types of experiences. Hearing for most persons is a passive activity not requiring much participation from the learner. Also, hearing is very selective. We tend to hear what we want to hear.

Another category of teaching activities is the use of visual symbols. **Visual symbols** involve the learner through the sense of seeing. Activities in this category are: use of teaching pictures, film-strips, map study, seeing movies, looking at books, and many other types of visual presentations. Most persons learn more from what they see than from what they hear. Seeing is less passive than hearing. Seeing elicits a response from the one who sees. When verbal and visual symbols are used together in a combined activity, the learning is more effective than when either is used separately.

Simulated Experiences move us a step farther than verbal and visual activities. To simulate is to act out, to act as if it is real but it is not actually real. Teaching activities in this category are role playing, dramatics, simulation games, some field trips, some creative writing and other experiences which place students in the position of acting out particular feelings, problems, or issues. An example of a creative writing simulated experience would be where a student assumes the role of Moses at the time he has returned to Egypt to seek freedom for the Hebrew slaves. Moses has confronted Pharoah, who has refused to let the people go and instead has increased their work load. Pharoah is uncooperative. The Hebrew people are angry at Moses and Moses wonders whether or not God is going to keep his promise. That is the situation to be simulated. The students are directed to write a letter, as Moses would write, to his wife, father-in-law, or friend back in Midian. A simulated activity involves the students more significantly in developing and identifying with the concepts of the session.

Direct Experiences are those activities when students are actually involved in "for real" situations, problems, and concepts. Because so many concepts in religious teaching tend to be abstract it is often difficult to design direct experience teaching activities.

An example in working on the concept of "love your neighbor as yourself" would be for the students to visit a Convalescent Home or other shut-ins to share with persons some moments of friendship and joy.

We can talk about "love your neighbor" in a long discussion and chances are it will make little impression. We could select pictures from magazines to illustrate examples of persons loving other persons and the meaning would be more memorable. We could act out or write endings to several open-ended stories illustrating persons needing love and this gets closer to the meaning of the concept. And, we could go as a class, or in small groups, to visit some persons who really need love from a neighbor. Which activity would require the most involvement on the part of the student? What activity would be most memorable? My hunch is that visiting some shut-ins could be remembered by some students for a life-time. Also, the next time the students hear "and you shall love your neighbor as yourself" they will have a specific experience to use as a frame of reference for relating to the concepts of love and neighbor.

A *FOURTH STEP* in the planning process involves deciding on the **sequence** in which the activities will occur.

Every lesson plan has a beginning, middle, and end. There are many alternative activities that are appropriate for beginning, developing and ending a lesson. In what follows there are several parts of the typical lesson plan that are identified specifically.

1. **Opening the Session** - The first thing that teachers and students do in a session is one of the most important activities of the whole hour. The opening segment could be as brief as one minute or as long as ten minutes.

2. **Presenting the Subject** - Before students can engage in purposeful study it is helpful to present to them some of the basic information related to the concepts to be developed in the session.

3. **Exploring the Subject** - Students are more motivated for learning when they are able to work individually or in small groups to explore further the subject matter that is the focus of the day's session.

4. **Responding Creatively** - Learning is reinforced and students are able to express themselves in meaningful ways when they are encouraged to respond in one or more creative ways to what they have learned.

5. **Concluding the Session** - Each session should be brought to a fitting conclusion so that students sense a completeness to the sequence of learning activities experienced that day.

All teacher's manuals include the above five categories whether or not they are identified by the same titles. Even though there is something of a logical sequence to these five parts of a lesson plan it is possible that the Presenting, Exploring and Responding activities could be experienced in a variety of combinations. It is possible that Presenting and Exploring activities could happen simultaneously as when students are researching a subject using a variety of resources. Also, Exploring and Responding activities may happen together as when students are writing their own script for selected frames of a filmstrip.

There are many, many different teaching-learning activities that can be used in each of the above five parts of a lesson plan.

A *FIFTH STEP* is to select resources that will be used to implement whatever teaching activities are planned.

Teaching-learning **activities** are what teachers and students **do** in and out of the classroom to experience and communicate particular concepts. **Resources** are what teachers and students **use** in the process of teaching and learning.

Resources may be organized in the same categories as described in the preceding section on teaching-learning activities. Some example of resources in each category are:

RESOURCES FOR **VERBAL** ACTIVITIES

- cassette tapes to listen to
- cassette recorder for recording students' statements
- phonograph player for listening to records
- pens or pencils and paper for writing activities
- resource books without diagrams, maps or photos with just words

RESOURCES FOR **VISUAL** ACTIVITIES

- maps, charts, posters, photographs and banners
- filmstrips and projectors
- overhead projector and transparencies
- 16mm films and projectors
- 8mm cameras, films and projectors
- chalk board, bulletin board, white board
- books with photographs, paintings, diagrams, maps
- magazine pictures
- 35mm cameras, slides, projectors
- write-on slides, filmstrips, and films
- flannel board, magnetic board

RESOURCES FOR **SIMULATED** ACTIVITIES

- puppets and stage for puppet plays
- directions and supplies for simulation games
- scripts, props, costumes, etc., for dramas
- materials for constructing some scale models
- resources for motivating, presenting, and responding in ways that help students identify with a person, event, or concept.

RESOURCES FOR **DIRECT EXPERIENCE** ACTIVITIES

- All the above resources could be used to help students do something directly related to key concepts that are connected with his own life experience.

- In addition there are many, many resources that can help students experience learning directly.

Teachers gather resources from many places: closets at home, cupboards at church, local stores, denominational offices and publishers, and even the trash can.

Resources can be as costly as a video-tape system and as inexpensive as a magazine.

If students are to be motivated to become involved in the process of their learning and if they are to use more than verbal symbols to express themselves, then teachers need to use a wide variety of resources.

Resources are as necessary to teaching and learning as dishes and utensils are to eating. You can survive without resources - but not without experiencing considerable frustration.

There are many books, magazines, and articles that suggest creative uses of a wide variety of resources.

Many teachers have experienced great excitement and satisfaction as they have become involved with other teachers in brainstorming possible ways to use a particular resource.

CRITERIA FOR EVALUATING LESSON PLANS

After you have created your session plan you could use the following criteria as a basis for evaluating those plans. In the list of criteria you will first read a question that should be asked of your lesson plan, then there is a brief commentary on that question to help you in your evaluation.

1. *Is the main idea limited to a few key concepts?*

   One of the important aspects of planning for teaching is to limit the number of concepts to be communicated in one session. It is possible for the **teacher** to "cover" a lot of concepts in one session, but it is much more important for the **students** to participate in "uncovering" a few key concepts. Keep the concepts connected to each other and related to the life experiences of the students.

2. *Are the main ideas and objectives appropriate for the age group?*

   With younger students it is more important to select appropriate parts of a story or event than it is to try to teach the whole story. We need to be sure the students have mastered some of the basic skills before expecting them to achieve more complex objectives. With older students we can deal with abstractions and symbols whereas younger students will be more limited by their concrete thinking.

3. *Are the main ideas and objectives directly connected?*

   It is not surprising to find situations where main ideas and objectives are not directly related to each other. For instance, teachers often select a main idea related to slavery of the Hebrews in Egypt and then select an objective focusing on contemporary forms and situations of slavery.

   Slavery is the only thing connecting the two, but the historical situations are three thousand years apart. If the main idea of the Hebrews as slaves in Egypt is introduced then the objective should be related to the main idea and not to contemporary forms of slavery. If that objective is intended then a related main idea should be selected. It would be possible to use both main ideas and both objectives even in the same session.

4. *Which types of teaching activities and resources are to be used?*

   In reviewing all the teaching activities and resources that are planned there should be a balance of verbal, visual, simulated and direct experiences. If there is a heavy use of just verbal activities and resources then the plan is out of balance. There needs to be a blending of all the different types of experiences.

5. *What kinds of questions did the teachers ask during the session?*

   There are at least three categories of questions which include information, analytical and personal questions. All three types of questions should be asked during the session. If there are more information questions than the other two categories, then the students are not being encouraged to think enough and apply the subject matter to their own lives.

6. *What choices did the students get to make during the session?*

   Every student should have the opportunity to make a number of choices during the sessions. Students are more motivated and more involved when they are encouraged to make choices during the session. Some choices are little, like deciding which book to read or which colors to use to express a feeling. Other choices may be big, like deciding how to interpret a passage of scripture or deciding how to act in a particular situation. Little or Big, students need many opportunities to make choices.

7. *Are there a variety of activities and resources planned for the session?*

A one activity lesson is a dull lesson. Students represent different abilities, interests, and needs so that teachers must plan for a variety of activities and resources in order to respond to the individual student differences. Students need a change of pace, they need to build from one activity to the next in order to maintain a high level of motivation.

8. *If the students are expected to do something new, have they had a chance to practice or experiment?*

Teachers should regularly introduce new activities and resources for the students to use in their exploring and creating. In order to insure the student's success with new activities and resources, there needs to be a time for practice and experimentation where students can find out for themselves how to do or use what the teacher has planned. The same principle applies to the teacher who plans to use a new resource or try a new activity. There needs to be time allowed for previewing, practicing and experimenting by the teacher.

9. *Has the room been arranged to facilitate the achievement of the intended objectives?*

Arrangement of tables and chairs; placement of learning centers, activity corners and resource equipment; display of visual materials on the wall, bulletin board or chalk board; and easy accessibility of all necessary supplies all contribute significantly to smooth functioning of the class and achievement of the intended objectives. Look at your room before the students arrive. What does the room say to you? It should speak very loudly of what is expected to happen in that session. The room arrangement needs to be changed regularly. sometimes as often as weekly.

10. *How much time will be required for each of the activities that is planned?*

The best lesson plan ever can be "shot-down" if sufficient time has not been allowed for each activity. Be realistic about time. Allow enough time for students to work without being rushed. Be flexible enough to adjust the schedule if necessary. Also, plan for some additional activities for those students who work more quickly or have more ability.

By applying these questions to the plans you have made it should be possible to evaluate what you have planned before trying to teach the plan. If you can discuss the plan with someone else you should be able to receive enough feedback for your responses to the questions to be realistic. Consider reworking some of your plans before you enter the classroom to teach them.

CUES TO INCREASE PARTICIPATION AND INTERACTION

A program of generations learning together will not work unless the leaders are able to develop and practice some very basic, effective communication skills. Persons who can teach adults or other persons who are effective as teachers of children, or youth, are not necessarily competent and comfortable in a teaching-learning setting that involves persons representing several ages and stages of growth. However, a teacher who is an effective communicator with one age group may, with some training and practice, develop the skills necessary to work with intergenerational groups.

There are some very basic principles of communication which can be implemented in any class, no matter what the age group. It is especially important that these principles be practiced where several age groups are together. The principles will be represented as a series of **cues** which are outlined below. The reason for practicing these cues is in order to increase the participation and interaction of **all** the members of the group.

CUE 1 - Leaders are Not Necessarily Experts

To volunteer to be a leader for an intergenerational group that will spend time together in a variety of learning activities does not require that one be an expert in specific subject matter or even in group processes. The leader needs to be one who has time to spend planning, who enjoys persons of all ages, who is sensitive to the needs and interests of others and who is open to the ideas and expressions of others.

CUE 2 - Persons Have Names

Leaders need to call on persons and refer to persons by name. This not only reinforces the person but also sets a model for others to follow. Children and others who have a hard time remembering names will be helped when they hear the names of persons repeated. Name tags may be helpful at the beginning, but it is important to really learn persons names and not continually depend upon the name tag.

The leaders and/or group will have to decide early how children will address the adults by name. Some groups feel strongly that everyone should be addressed by their first name by all ages. Others feel just as strongly that children should address adults by Mr. Mrs., and Miss.

CUE 3 - Families Don't Always Have to Stay Together

For some activities, and for some families, it will be important for the family to stay together. It may be important during the first couple of sessions that families be together. However, one of the values of generations learning together is the opportunity for persons of all ages to encounter others from different age groups, different family customs, and different personal interest. Children, especially, need to interact with adults other than their parents. And, single persons, older adults and others without families present in the community need the enrichment that comes to their lives from relationships with others of all ages.

Plan activities that provide for occasional opportunities for persons to regroup themselves in other than family groups.

CUE 4 - Balance Individual, Small and Large Group Activities

A session that is totally devoted to large group activities or emphasizes only small group activities is a session that is out of balance. One session may feature one type of activity more than another, but there should always be some individual, some small group and some large group activities during a session, or series of sessions.

ACTIVITY	ADVANTAGES	DISADVANTANGES
Individual Activities	- Persons can work at his/her own pace. - Person can choose what is of personal interest. - Leader may be able to seek opportunity to relate to individual.	- No opportunity for interaction with others. - Person is not challenged by ideas and feelings of others.
Small Group Activity	- Persons are more involved with each other. - Exposure to different ideas, feelings, values. - Develop skills of cooperation, negotiation and planning.	- Assertive, verbal person may dominate. - If adults become leaders children may withdraw, depending on sensitivity of the leader. - May take a lot of time.
Large Group Activity	- Takes less total time - Everyone experiences the same thing. - The best way to present films, filmstrips, and other "input" activites. - Worship, games, meals, simulation activities and other similar experiences work well when the whole group is together.	- The quieter, less verbal persons get lost in the group. - Hard for leader to be aware of how all persons are responding. - Persons may not be able to make their own choices about what and how to do. - Individuals may lose interest.

CUE 5 - Choices Increase Motivation

Persons who are able to **make choices** about what and how they are going to learn, and with whom they are to do it, are more motivated than those who are **told** what to do. When we have persons with so many different abilities, interests, and needs as we have in an intergenerational setting it is especially important that we plan for persons to make as many choices as possible.

Persons can make choices when they....

    ...decide where to sit.
    ...select which person with whom to work.
    ...choose which materials to use in order to do a creative activity.

...state answers to questions in their own words.
...decide which resource books to use in their study.
...elect which learning center or activity to work at.
...choose a role with which to identify.
...rank items in their own personal order of priority.
...decide which scripture passages to read or which Bible to use.

CUE 6 - Provide a Common Starting Place

Leaders will be helpful to both younger and older learners if a common starting place is provided for all to experience together. It is better to not assume that the participants already have prior knowledge or experience. Even if a subject is presented that is familiar to a few persons, it may be that they will still get some new insights or find that what they knew previously is being reinforced.

A common starting place may be....

...a passage of scripture read by leader or individually.
...a film or filmstrip
...a verbal presentation
...a series of questions or activities on a worksheet.
...a story which is told or read or acted out.
...something on a cassette recording for all to hear.
...a photograph, painting, teaching picture or other visual.
...a definition from a book or printed on a chart.
...tasks outlined in a worksheet.
...words from a song, poem, or speech.

CUE 7 - Be Sure Instructions Are Clear

With persons representing a wide range of abilities, interests and experiences some will need very clear, step by step instructions for most activities. Others may need only a general suggestion of how to do an activity or what is expected. For the sake of the whole group it is important to provide simple, step by step, clearly stated instructions. Instructions are best when they are written so that everyone can read and then work at their own pace. Write instructions on newsprint, poster board, chalk board, mimeograph sheet, or overhead transparency.

CUE 8 - Make It Visible

Persons can comprehend much more when they can **see** as well as **hear**. Charts, diagrams, pictures, photographs, overhead projection, and other visual presentations are very helpful. When listening to an unfamiliar song it is helpful to have the words printed so all can read while listening. When presenting a biblical story it will help both adults and children to focus on the story through a film, filmstrip, or teaching picture that presents the story visually.

CUE 9 - Everyone Can Be Creative

To be creative does not mean that one has to be an artist. It does mean that one has some ideas and feelings that are personal and special that can be expressed in any of several dozen creative ways. The leaders do not need to be creative with music, painting, writing, or drama in order to facilitate others expressing themselves in those creative media. The leaders only need to provide the setting, the materials, and the motivation so that others can choose which medium to use in order to create their own verbal, visual, or enacted expressions.

Creative activities are not busy-work. Creative activities are the means by which persons express their own personal affirmations of what they think, feel, believe and value.

CUE 10 - Share What Has Been Created

There is value for a person just in the **process** of creating, but there is increased value for that person and others in the group when what was created is **shared**. The sharing may be with the whole group as part of a closing presentation, or it may be with one or a few persons in an informal way. Creative expressions can be shared by mounting on a display board, reproducing on a mimeograph or displaying on a table.

CUE 11 - Don't Be Afraid of Feelings

Much Christian education tends to focus on facts, doctrines, events, and interpretations. This can all be interesting but it may never reach the emotional and affective aspects of a person's life. Feelings are universal. We can connect with Biblical persons more directly at the feeling level than at any other. We can come closer to other persons in our group when we share our feelings with each other. There may be times when strong feelings get expressed in a group that cause us to be somewhat uncomfortable. However, better to risk being uncomfortable than to suppress or neglect the importance of sharing at the feeling level.

CUE 12 - Accept Ideas and Feelings

When teachers, leaders and others are able to accept the ideas or feelings expressed by persons in the group there is much more opportunity for interaction. We can **accept** ideas and feelings expressed by others without necessarily having to **agree** with them. When persons sense they are accepted they are much more willing and able to participate. We can show our acceptance in several ways:

- non-verbally with a smile, nod, or other gesture.
- by reflecting back what a person has said.
- by asking persons to clarify what they meant by what they said.
- by identifying with them through reflecting on our own personal experiences that are similar.

CUE 13 - Ask Open Questions

Closed questions have right and wrong answers. Answering closed questions feels like taking a test. It is impossible to have a discussion with closed questions. Information is important but it can be presented in many ways without having to ask a series of closed, informational questions.

Open questions lead to discussion. Open questions require more in the way of analytical thinking and personalized application. There are usually a variety of possible "right answers" to an open question. Open questions are prefaced by phrases such as:

"Why do you suppose...."
"What are some possibilities of..."
"How does that compare with..."
"Why do you think..."
"What are some examples of..."
"What is an occasion when..."
"When you think of _____ what comes to mind..."
"What would you think if..."
"How would you act in the situation of..."

CUE 14 - Ask for Clarification

If a person answers a question or makes a statement with a very brief response you will almost always be safe in assuming that the person has more to offer than the brief statement. The teacher-leader can respond to the brief statement with a request that the student say a little more, clarify, expand on his original statement. More times than not the person will have more to say.

Also, there are times when a student answers a question or makes a statement and we do not understand what was meant. Here again we can ask for clarification, "Say a little more what you meant by..." or, "I don't quite understand, help me to see what you mean by..."

Leaders need to be sensitive to adult answers and statements and ask for clarification sometimes not because the **leader** does not understand, but because there is the possibility that the **children** may not understand. This is especially true in the beginning when children may be hesitant to admit they don't understand or to ask questions. Adults need to be reminded to express themselves so that **everyone** understands them.

CUE 15 - Listening is Important

Teachers and Leaders need to listen as much as, or perhaps even more than the participants in their groups. Instead of being anxious about what we want to tell or ask the other person it will be better to just listen to what the other is saying and then after listening figure out a way to respond. Persons will know we are listening when we look directly at them and are not distracted with other interests and when we respond in non-verbal or verbal ways that communicate we hear them. In intergenerational groups leaders will have to work hard at helping children to listen to adults and especially for adults to really listen to children.

CUE 16 - Silence is Okay

If the leader asks a good, open question and there is not an immediate response the worst thing the leader can do is to break the silence with an answer, or with more questions. If it is a good question it will take time to think through an answer. Ten to fifteen seconds is not a very long time for thinking. Yet, the average teacher cannot tolerate more than five seconds of silence after a question. Silence is okay. Let the participants "feel the burden" of the silence. They will respond when they realize they are responsible for the silence instead of waiting for the leader to break the silence.

CUE 17 - Everyone Has A Right to "Pass"

There is no special virture in having all participants speak up or express themselves everytime there is an opportunity. It is especially disturbing to go around the circle expecting every person to share something in turn. The poor person who is tenth in line had six good ideas but they were all shared before his turn. That person feels as if he/she has failed. Instead the teacher is the one who failed by setting up the activity in that way. Persons should have the right to "pass", to not share anything if they choose not to. In their choosing not to share they should not be made to feel as if they have failed. It is better to ask a question or offer a task to the whole group than to go around the circle or call on one specific person.

GETTING STARTED WITH A GROUP

Even though we live in families, which are by nature intergenerational, most of us do not have many experiences where children, youth and adults are all involved in a program where each is a participant with equal standing and responsibility. Since this may be a new experience for most persons it is very important that the groups get started in such a way that everyone feels a part of the group. "Getting started" activities will help establish the feeling tone of the whole program. Several things can be achieved by effective "getting started" activities:

- Persons will become involved quickly in a non-threatening, fun way.
- Persons will begin to get acquainted with each other.
- A style of leadership and participation will be established.
- Persons of various ages will have opportunity to "mix it up" with each other.

The leader needs to be as relaxed and flexible as possible when getting started with a group. This is asking alot, because most leaders will be very anxious about the first couple of sessions with a new group and a new type of program. However, if the planning has been carefully and thoroughly done the leader can be free to respond to the persons in the group and their needs, showing confidence in the process and the plans that have been made. This confidence will facilitate an atmosphere of trust and will lead the whole group to a state of relaxation about the class. After a few weeks when this level is reached the leader and participants may want to talk about their feelings toward the whole program.

When selecting a "getting started" activity the leader should pick one that he/she feels good about. The process of the activity should be clear, the directions should be well thought out, and some problems may be anticipated along with responses to the problems. Select an activity that you feel confident will work with your particular group.

Some possible "getting started" activities are:

A. Match Facts to Persons

1. Give each person 3 or 4 3x5 cards or similar size pieces of paper. Each person also needs a pencil.

2. Instruct each person to write something different on each card that would tell a fact about himself/herself. Some suggested categories are: a hobby, a place visited, a funny experience, something about a trip or vacation, favorite pet or sport, or something else. Write a different fact on each card. Younger children may need help from parents.

3. After all the cards are completed everyone places all their cards in a pile in the center of the room. Turn cards upside down and scramble them.

4. Then, each person draw out of the pile as many cards as they put in. If you draw your own card, put it back and draw another.

5. Now, circulate among the group trying to find the persons to whom the cards belong. This usually takes some time. And, this is where a lot of brief, informal visiting happens. Younger children may need a little extra encouragement to get started. Encourage them to feel free to approach adults as well as other children.

6. When a person finds a match to the card write that person's name on the card so that the information can be used to introduce the person later.

7. After everyone has identified the "owners" of their cards sit in a circle and begin to introduce persons one by one.

8. The leader will have a roster of all the members of the group. Read one name at a time. Persons who have cards with information about the person whose name was read will read the information on the cards and share any other bits of information about that person.

The value of this process is that everyone is involved in a personal way, encountering all the persons in the group in brief, one-to-one encounters. Persons decide for themselves what they want to share with the whole group about themselves. And, with such a variety of personal anecdotes being presented persons in the group will identify others with whom they may want to have further conversation.

Don't rush this getting acquainted process. It is important!

B. Circle Within A Circle

1. Organize the total group into two circles, one circle will stand inside the other circle. The two circles should have equal numbers of persons.

2. The inside circle turns around to face the outside circle which means that each person should be standing face to face with another person. If there is an uneven number in the group then the leader can participate to make the circles even.

3. The leader says something like, "The outside circle move three persons to the left and talk for one minute about where you were born."

4. This process is repeated for as many times as the leader chooses. Move "x" number of spaces to left or right so that each time persons end up face to face with someone different.

5. Some possible topics for quick conversation are:

   - What is your favorite TV Show?
   - One thing you did this last summer.
   - What musical instrument do you play or like the best?
   - One vegetable you don't like and one you do like.
   - Someone who is a hero to you.
   - A place in the world you would like to visit.
   - A famous person you would like to meet.
   - A favorite place to eat away from home.
   - If you had $100.00 what is something you would buy?
   (Keep the conversations limited to one minute each.)

C. Choose What You Like

1. Leader introduces the activity by giving an example "When I mention two things, like sailing or surfing, which would you like to do most, go sailing on a lake or go surfing in the ocean?"

2. Each person chooses one of the other of the alternatives.

3. Leader identifies one side of the room for one choice and the other side for the other choice.

4. Persons go to the side of the room which represents their choice.

5. Each person meets with one other person who made the same choice.

6. For one minute each they share with each other why they chose that particular item.

7. Then the leader calls, "time" and gives another pair of items from which persons must choose one. Some examples of other choices are:

   - Eating at McDonalds **or** Holiday Inn.
   - Hiking in the Mountains **or** cycling along a highway

- Working in an ice-cream parlor **or** toy store
- Spending time at a library **or** museum
- Going to a potluck supper **or** progressive dinner
- Taking a trip on a plane **or** a boat
- Visiting friends in the city **or** on a farm

D. People Scavenger Hunt

1. Leader prepares a list on a ditto sheet that **represents the kinds of things we may be able to** find out about other persons.

2. Each participant receives a list for the scavenger hunt and then tries to find someone who would represent that item.

3. When someone is found who matches the item their name is written in the blank space.

4. Persons try to fill in all of the blanks in the time that is given.

5. When the leader calls "time" the group gathers. The leader reads off each item. Everyone who has a name in that blank reads the name and then the person whose name is called stands up. if anyone else thinks that item "fits" them, they can call out their name and stand up also.

6. A sample list of items (make up your own to be appropriate for your group).

   Find:

   a. Someone with hazel eyes _____

   b. An oldest child in the family _____

   c. The tallest person in the group _____

   d. The person with the longest last name _____

   e. A person born outside the United States _____

   f. A person whose first name begins with "C" _____

   g. One of the leaders of the group _____

   h. A person who is a Yankees fan _____

   i. A person born in this town _____

   j. A person who likes to read _____

   k. A person wearing glasses _____

   l. Someone who plays a piano _____

   m. Someone who likes to watch sports on TV _____

   n. An adult who walked a mile to school as a child _____

   o. The youngest person who is an aunt or uncle _____

   p. A person who likes to play tennis _____

   q. The person with the shortest first name _____

   r. Someone who likes to eat pizza _____

s. Someone who owns a CB radio _____

t. A child who walks the farthest to school _____

u.

v.

w. (add some of your own)

x.

y.

z.

A TRAINING EVENT FOR PROSPECTIVE LEADERS

It is possible that a church, cluster of churches or denominational group will want to plan a training event for prospective leaders. The outline which follows is from a six-hour workshop which Don has conducted several times. This outline is presented to serve only as a sample of what is possible. It is important for each planning group to design their own workshop to respond to the interests and needs of the persons in their group.

GENERATIONS LEARNING TOGETHER
(A sample 6 hour Workshop)

The Opening

A. Greeting of persons and introductions

B. A get acquainted activity - in groups of three to five - share with each other something you have enjoyed doing where more than one generation was involved.

C. Each small group write down the experiences the persons mentioned. Write a phrase about each on a piece of newsprint. Mount the newsprint on the wall.

D. Spend a few minutes where everyone will browse among the lists of experiences that are mounted.

Introductory Presentation

Leader will offer some brief comments that may include references to...

A. A developing, widespread interest in family clusters and other intergenerational activities in churches.

B. Decline, disruption and disintegration of the family in America - especially the extended family, also the nuclear family.

C. Church **tends to be** a place and program that separates family members, and age groups, from each other.

D. Church **can be** a place and program that brings families, and age groups, together in learning, worship, fellowship and service activities.

E. Some personal experiences and impressions.

Film Showing

A film was produced based on the Reformed Church in America Family Festival '72. It is a beautiful film which is well produced and captures the essence of what happened at the Family Festival. The film is not dated however, and is not a documentary of one event. There are many timeless, relevant aspects of the film which will make it appropriate as long as there are families in the church.

I like to use the film because of the concepts of family that are presented and because of the "feeling tone" it establishes. Also, we see in the film many examples of generations learning, worshipping, and sharing together.

Before presenting the film I ask persons to look for something specific.

> *Look for principles of learning and interaction that suggest important concerns related to generations learning together.*

The showing of the film is followed by a discussion which begins with a question such as:

> *What insights did you gain that would help you in your thinking about and planning for generations learning together.*

If the group is fairly small it can stay together to discuss the film. However, if the group is 20 persons or more it may be best to discuss in smaller groups.

Brainstorm Life-Centered Experiences

Activities planned for intergenerational groups must focus on life-centered experiences if we are going to involve in a meaningful way all ages of persons.

A. In two minutes - individually - write down words or phrases that represent personal, family, community, or church experiences that are common to persons of all ages. (These are what we mean by life-centered experiences.) They can be used as a basis for planning "curriculum" for intergenerational groups.

B. Each person select the two or three most important experiences on his/her list.

C. In small groups of three to five persons compare and share the top two or three experiences of each person.

D. Develop a composite list by having persons mention their experiences that they shared. The workshop leader write them all down on newsprint or overhead projection to form a composite list that the group can focus on.

E. Leader can make a few comments to summarize what is included on the composite list. Or, perhaps someone in the group will have some comments to make.

Samples of Life-Centered Experiences Mentioned by One Group:

family	friends	meals	school	birth
death	work	vacation	home	traveling
losing	leading	gifts	memories	enemies
reunions	pets	birthday	following	anniversaries
games	church	children	parties	winning
parents	mistakes	wind/rain/snow		

Planning for Generations Learning Together

Work in small groups of two or three persons.

Leader introduces one step at a time. Explain what is expected at each step. Be sure that instructions for each step are visible on a chart or transparency so that persons will have something to refer to while they are working.

Step 1   Select **one** life-centered experience from the composite list to be the focus for your planning.

Step 2	Explore in Bibles and other resource books for some biblical-theological reference points.
Step 3	Write a paragraph that states what you think is central to the experience and how it connects to the Christian life.
Step 4	Write out several objectives that you would intend for participants to accomplish as a result of spending time focusing on the subject.
Step 5	Brainstorm some possible activities and resources for involving persons to experience what you want to communicate.
Step 6	Plan a strategy that includes opening - exploring - creating - closing activities.
Step 7	Write all you have written on a ditto master so that it can be duplicated and shared with the whole group.

Some time needs to be spent reflecting on the whole process of planning as experienced in the above seven steps. It usually takes about an hour and a half to accomplish all seven steps.

A Sample Session of Generations Learning Together

About 10-12 children and youth of various ages need to be recruited ahead of time. Also, 10-12 persons from the workshop group need to be recruited to participate with the children and youth in a sample session of learning activities.

The others in the workshop group can be observers. They should scatter themselves throughout the room. As observers they should remain silent during the entire session. They can take notes to guide their comments and question asking after the sample session.

It is possible that this part of the workshop could happen earlier in the day. It all depends upon the times of the day the children and youth are available.

The content for the sample session can be taken from one of the session outlines in this book or from another source. It should be simple enough to do in an hour and representative enough to include a variety of aspects of the whole process of generations learning together. Also, the sample session has to be complete in and of itself.

Be sure to include a brief getting acquainted time at the beginning of the session because you will be working with a lot of strangers.

Reflection and Discussion

The following questions could guide a discussion that follows the sample session.

A. What did you see happen?

B. What are some problems with this style? What are the implications of those problems?

C. What are some values of this style and structure of teaching and learning?

D. What is the role of the teacher-leader?

E. What is the relation between what was demonstrated and the earlier experience of planning focused on a life-centered experience?

F. If you were to begin planning for this type of teaching-learning in your church
    - what are some questions you would have?
    - what are some first steps you would take?

G. What is a strategy for guiding some persons in the church to develop a program of generations learning together?

PART II:
FORMATION OF CHRISTIAN SELF-IDENTITY

We can become expert in the skills of planning, communicating and teaching. We can design an exciting program of christian education in the church. We can do a lot of things. But, unless we consider some of the basic principles and goals that underly all our planning and doing, we may not achieve what we had hoped or we may be disappointed in what was experienced by the persons for whom we were planning.

Perhaps one of the root questions that each of us who plans for teaching in the church should respond to is, "How is Christian self-identity formed?" There are many possible responses to that question. I am sure most of us respond first out of our own personal experiences. That is important, but it is not enough. We need to consider what others think and we need to reflect on the experiences of others both from the biblical-historical perspective and from the present.

It is very important for us to reflect on the formation of Christian self-identity because it seems to me that that is the heart of the whole ministry of education in the church - the influencing of persons in the formation of their Christian self-identity. My reflecting in this article is just one way to respond. Each of us needs to deal with the subject in our own way.

I think I am a product of a church that represented a style of nurture that was presented by Horace Bushnell in his classic book, CHRISTIAN NURTURE. He wrote,

"A child is to grow up a Christian and never know himself as being otherwise."

That is true for me. I do not remember a time what I was not a part of the Christian community, thinking of myself as a Christian. I went to Sunday School, Vacation Bible School, Communicants Class, Youth Fellowship, Church Worship, and the Boy Scouts. Yes, Boy Scouts in my experience was part of the church just like Sunday School and Youth Fellowship. I thought of myself as Christian. Didn't everybody?

I can remember being surprised and confused at the first evangelistic service I attended when I was in the ninth grade. The evangelist was very dynamic and seemed to know all the answers about the christian life. He caused me to wonder about my church experience and to question whether my faith was sincere enough. I realized that I had never made the kind of decision he was calling for. Yes, I walked forward. I participated in a brief period of counsel and prayer. Then I went home. I continued to be active in the church. I seemed more sure that I was a Christian. But, the experience never seemed dramatic enough to qualify for the kind of "being born again" that seemed so important to those who pushed their religion at me in high school and college. As an adult I reflect back on my adolescent experiences and I realize that Christian self-identity is not formed by just one event in a person's life. One event may be a turning point or it may be a highlight, but one event does not form the whole life.

The formation of Christian self-identity is a result of a pilgrimage - a pilgrimage that involves a whole life-time of experiences. Our parents are a significant part of that pilgrimage. The church community through pastors, teachers, leaders, groups, activities, programs, projects, and everything else contributes to the formation of who we are. Friends and other peers at all stages of our lives share with us their values, their dreams and their reactions to us and in this way contribute to who we become. In, through, and beyond all these influences there is the power and presence of God at work in our lives through his Holy Spirit.

Our experiences with family, church community, friends, and God are remembered as we focus on events or shared experiences. C. Ellis Nelson in his book **WHERE FAITH BEGINS** writes,

"We experience reality in events, a unit of meaning which combines persons and circumstances. Learning takes place according to a person's participation in events. We are conditioned by awareness of what is happening, by our own personal characteristics and abilities, and by the perceptual system that has been built into us by our culture. God is known in what happens rather than in speculative reason. The Biblical record is primarily a description of events and the meaning of these events for a believing community."

(pp 93-94)

Christian self-identity is formed when we recognize that God is present not only in the events of history, but also in the events of our personal and corporate lives. Events in history and in our lives and the interpretations of those events are what contribute to the making of tradition. Tradition is a body of belief communicated from past generations to the present. Tradition results from the process of hearing, remembering, affirming and retelling the story of our origins as a religion, as a nation or as a family. Traditions are shared, acted out, expressed visually, celebrated in dance, festival and worship, and composed in narrative, poetic and musical forms. We know ourselves and are known by others according to the stories we create, remember, and tell about who and whose we are. We are shaped by the traditions with which we identify and we reshape those traditions as we pass them on to others.

When we know and affirm the story of our people and experience ourselves as being part of that story then we are in a position to be a link in the process of passing the tradition from one generation to the next. Tradition is maintained more by respect than by legal authority and is a strong stabilizing force resisting change. However, times change, nations change, persons change so that traditions change also. It is not just a matter of inaugurating new traditions but rather a transforming of old traditions to accommodate them for ourselves in a new time. Persons and communities who transform a tradition of the past are not negating the tradition but rather are affirming the value of the tradition as they attempt to interpret it and implement it in terms of their present time.

If there had not been a tradition, a story, there would not have been a people of the old covenant, Israel, or of the new covenant, the Body of Christ. Central to the life of God's people in every generation was the remembering and retelling of God's actions on their behalf. Important events in the life of the people (creation, flood, covenant making, exodus, wars of victory and defeat, exile and return, the birth, life, death, and resurrection of a Savior and the formation of a believing community) were all identified as times when God was acting in, for, through the affairs of his people. The stories of God at work for his people and the people's relationships with God and with others, were formed, told, remembered and retold to such an extent that events in centuries past became a part of one's own personal story. To the Hebrew person of a later time the account of "A wandering Aramean was my father; and he went down into Egypt..." (Deut. 26:5) was not just the telling about Joseph's father, but in a very real sense it was the story of his father.

It is very important to reflect on events and persons in history to discern what God is doing and meaning in those events. It is also important to cause events to happen in our churches, communities, and families in order that God may be at work in and through us. Present events for Christians are part of a tradition. It is tradition that links the past to the present. Christian identity will be formed in part as a result of a person's participation in and reflection upon the events, and the traditions, of the community of faith, the church.

Persons do not exist by themselves as autonomous persons. They are influenced, encouraged and supported as individuals by the groups with which they associate. It is in their associations with family, school, work, play, neighborhood, club and church that persons' values, loyalties, dreams and goals are influenced which in turn help form self-identity.

The primary groups to which persons belong are very important in the formation of self-identity. Perhaps the church has an essential role in providing the framework of concepts, values, commitments, and experiences by which persons judge the purpose of the other groups of which they are members and the degree of their allegence to those groups. Instead of being apologetic in our approaches to persons to associate with the church and its groups, the church should be more assertive in terms of what it represents and what it expects from its members.

For the church to exert primary influence upon persons it is necessary that significant amounts of energy, time and other personal resources be committed to its life. The church cannot be the church on fringes of commitment of tired, over-extended persons. There needs to be a balance. It is not that the church should become one's whole life, but rather that the traditions, the beliefs, the values, and the events of the church's life become the measuring rod by which all other associations and events are measured.

The formation of Christian self-identity is a growing process rather than a finished product. The process is dynamic, changing, transforming. The old person is continually passing away in order that the new person may be born. The process is not just a matter of accumulated wisdom, classical creeds, and correct beliefs. Rather, the process involves persons interacting with persons in the midst of events involving their lives together.

When I think of the growing, learning, forming of Christian identity I think of a **process** that involves a variety of components. Focus for example on one of the key words and experiences of the Christian faith - **FORGIVENESS**.

A. To start with FORGIVENESS is a word - a **symbol** that represents a real experience, an event, involving persons and God.

- I can learn a prayer that includes the words "Forgive us our debts as we forgive our debtors"

- I can hear, read, and even remember a parable that Jesus tells in response to Peter's question: "Lord, how many times can my brother sin against me and I have to forgive him? Seven times?" (Matt. 18:21-35)

This is a part of the formation of Christian identity but only a part, a small part.

B. To communicate the concept and act of forgiveness we might **retell** the story in a dramatic way or we might present some visual images to **show** the meaning and drama of the parable of the unforgiving servant.

- A person can respond emotionally to the story or the visuals.

- The person may remember the story better as a result of visualizing it.

And, we have another small part of the process of formation of Christian identity.

C. Through discussion led by a perceptive, helpful teacher persons can be led to **analyze** and **interpret** the parable and its appropriateness for communicating forgiveness.

- The discussion and analysis may be interesting and challenging.

- Persons ideas and feelings may be expressed honestly and affectionately.

And, forgiveness comes closer to the reality of a person's experiences.

D. In the process of hearing, seeing, discussing, and analyzing forgiveness and the parable persons may become able to **restate** the parable in their own creative words or they may be able to recreate through some expressive medium their understanding of the parable.

- Through these verbal and visual restatements of the parable persons will have invested significant aspects of themselves.

- They will have shared aspects of their own experiences and personalities that may have previously been hidden.

- Their tuning-in to the essence of the parable can be enhanced by such involvement.

Thus, another step in the process of appropriating the concept and experience of forgiveness for their own lives.

E. By involving persons in **identifying** with the circumstances, feelings, and action of the story of the Unforgiving Servant it is possible that they will be able to act out, speak out as if they were experiencing the parable.

- When individuals can identify with persons, events, concepts they come closer to the reality than just thinking, talking or seeing.

- To identify with an event or person from another time or culture is to bridge the chasm between that time and the present.

This too is another aspect that contributes to the formation of Christian self-identity.

F. Another experience that contributes to persons' self-identity formation is when they can **apply** concepts and events from another source to their own lives. This application happens:

- When they recognize something happening in a relationship that is similar to what they remember from the context of the parable.

- When they are guided by discussion, reading, or thinking to recall previous experiences that are similar to the point of the parable.

- When they can project future experiences that might call upon them to act as one who forgives the way the king forgave in the parable.

One more contribution is made to the influencing of forgiveness to become a part of one's life and faith.

G. Of course one has not learned what forgiveness means or how to forgive or how to accept forgiveness until he/she **acts** in a way that forgiving and accepting forgiveness become operational in his/her everyday behavior and relationships.

- To pray the prayer, to recite the parable, to talk about forgiveness, or even to identify with others is not enough.

- Forgiveness, a forgiving nature, to offer forgiveness, to receive forgiveness involve acting, living, doing.

- Then learning happens. Then one aspect of Christian Self-identity is formed.

But, there is more to the process.

H. Becoming a forgiving person is not something I can will myself to be or instruct someone else to be. And, when I experience a moment of forgiveness it can easily be corrupted, misunderstood, or misappropriated. I cannot be complete or perfect. I am growing. I can be sensitive. There is more to the experience than what I can cause to happen. Within the whole process, especially in the context of the life and ministry of the church, God is at work in persons. God is at work in events. How God works I do not know. That he is at work I do not doubt. Because God has shown his power to create, establish, forgive, redeem and heal in past events I can claim that same power for my present.

If the outline above does represent some of the dynamics of the growing, forming, learning process which results in Christian self-identity it seems that there are several implications for the church's ministry in general and our work with intergenerational groups in particular.

1. We must move from being satisfied with neat, abstract statements about concepts, events, and persons, to working harder at presenting and experiencing these as concretely as possible.

2. Ways must be found to enable persons to identify with and personalize concepts, persons, events, and issues, both past and present including the biblical, traditional and existential.

3. Persons need to be helped to consider real alternatives for action, to reflect on the consequences of various alternatives, and to choose actions that are consistent with their understanding of the tradition of their faith.

4. Presenting correct information is not enough. Reflecting on the information, analyzing and interpreting it, identifying with it and acting it out are necessary other steps.

5. There are many, many ways to communicate with persons and involve them in thinking, studying and acting. We must choose carefully and use effectively as wide a variety of media and methods as possible.

6. Opportunities must be provided for persons of all ages to make affirmations of what they believe, feel, and value. Affirming what we believe only at the time of confirmation or in the words of someone else is not enough.

   Persons of all ages and stages of life can be helped to make affirmations of their faith in little ways as well as significant ways. This is especially important in intergenerational settings where each affirmation of each person is of equal authenticity and value.

7. We must continually tell the story of our faith and life. And, persons need to be helped to claim The Story as their own story. We have to work hard at declaring what The Story is and how we are going to share it. By the continual telling, hearing, remembering and living of The Story, and making it my story I become a part of The Story. When I see myself as part of The Story it seems to me there is to a large extent the formation of Christian self-identity.

   "How do we keep our balance? I can tell you in one word - TRADITION! Because of our Traditions everyone here knows who he is, and what God expects him to do. Without our Traditions life would be as shaky as a fiddler on a roof." (from FIDDLER ON THE ROOF)

PART III:

LEARNING ACTIVITIES FOR
GENERATIONS LEARNING TOGETHER

In most places the successful experiences of generations learning together will be designed by a creative, committed planning team. The local planning team will be very familiar with the needs, interests, and abilities of their own people. They will know schedules, space allocations, available resources, and budget requirements of their church. All of these factors influence the planning for learning activities that involve several generations. It is our hope that the previous chapters will have provided some guidelines for those responsible for planning.

What follows is a series of outlines of possible learning activities that could be used and/or adapted by a planning team as they prepare for intergenerational learning in their church. These outlines are intended to be "starters" in the planning process. The activities as presented have been used by Don and Pat Griggs in a variety of settings. However, to be used by other persons in different settings it is very important that these activities be revised, adapted, tailored to fit the unique circumstances of the local situation.

Each outline of a unit of study includes several items:

A. **INTRODUCTION** In this section we will set the stage by focusing on the theme or main idea of the session with some words of orientation and description.

B. **OBJECTIVES** Each session or unit of sessions will include several objectives. The objectives are basic to planning and evaluation. Not all participants will achieve all objectives. Some objectives will be more appropriate for younger learners and other objectives are directed to older learners.

C. **MATERIALS NEEDED** All activities require some resources to be used by and with participants.

D. **SEQUENCE OF ACTIVITIES** Each session and unit will be outlined with a sequence of activities that develops the theme and seeks to involve all the participants in a variety of ways.

UNIT ONE....DEVELOPING BIBLE SKILLS

A. INTRODUCTION

This unit was used with a group of thirty persons. The youngest was six years old. There were about eight elementary and five youth and the rest were adults. There were nine families represented by one or more of their members. The unit was designed for persons with reading skills. So when a six year old child showed up we were surprised. The parents felt that their son would make out fine and would have a good time even though he could not read well. That proved to be true since there were a lot of filmstrips and books with stories and pictures. Also, the six year old was free to participate or not according to how he and his parents decided.

Since this unit depends upon reading skills, older learners were encouraged to team-up with younger learners to provide the skills that were necessary to complete the planned activities. Reading aloud, exchanging ideas, asking and answering questions, and searching together for information became the norm for the class. The learners of all ages became "teachers" for each other.

We believe that it is important for students in the church of all ages to develop skills that will help them in studying the Bible. Children receive Bibles in third or fourth grade in many churches. Parents and youth have often either not learned basic Bible Skills or have not practiced them in order to maintain the skills. With this being true of persons in many churches, we think a unit focusing on Bible Skills can be very helpful and also a lot of fun. Our experience has been that all learners with abilities to read and to do some limited research are motivated to participate and receive much satisfaction from activities as outlined below.

B. UNIT OBJECTIVES

At the end of this unit participants should be able to:

1. Describe six to ten specific features of the Bible that make it different from other books.

2. Show another person how to use a Bible Concordance.

3. Find a passage of scripture by using cross-reference footnotes.

4. Find a key word in a Bible Dictionary and write or state a definition of that word in their own words.

5. Use Bible resource books to find information about persons and places in the Bible.

C. MATERIALS NEEDED

Bibles - RSV with study helps
Concise RSV Concordances
Bible Resource Books - Dictionaries, Atlases, Story Books, etc.
(see pages 51 and 52 for titles of books and information regarding where they are available.)
Pencils, Paper, Felt Pens, Construction Paper

D. SEQUENCE OF ACTIVITIES

This unit was prepared for a week-end family retreat. We had a total of five to six hours for the activities outlined here. To use this unit in a weekly setting of one hour sessions there must be some careful tailoring of the activities to fit the time, space, class, etc.

ACTIVITY ONE: GETTING ACQUAINTED

When we did this unit it was the first time for the group to be together. We spent the first fifteen minutes getting acquainted. We made name tags with "-ing words" on them and then used the "Circle in a Circle" activity. (see page 28 where some suggestions are offered for getting started with a group.)

ACTIVITY TWO: OBSERVATIONS OF THE BIBLE

Work in **family groups** or other **mixed age groups** of **three to five** persons.

Each person needs a Bible.

The leader can give the following instructions:

> *Look at the Bible. Flip through the pages. Make a list of the many things you notice about the Bible. Take five minutes to work as a group to make a list of as many observations as you can of what you notice about the Bible. There are no wrong answers.*

(Someone in each group should record on a piece of paper all the observations of the group.)

After five minutes the leader calls time then begins to make a composite list of Bible observations. Write the list on an overhead transparency, sheet of newsprint or chalkboard. Encourage groups to take turns in offering their observations so that each group will have equal opportunity to make their contributions.

The leader can then summarize by commenting on:

- How much the group knows about the Bible.
- How unique and different the Bible is from other books.
- How observant they were.

ACTIVITY THREE: QUESTIONS ABOUT THE BIBLE

Participants continue in the same small groups.

Each person writes on a slip of paper one or two questions about the Bible. Non-readers and beginning readers will have some questions even if they cannot write them down. Someone in each group should serve as a "scribe" for these students.

Groups exchange questions with each other. Each group reads their new set of questions and selects several questions to share with the whole class.

Make a composite list of questions from all the groups. Record questions on overhead transparency, chalkboard, or newsprint so that everyone can see all questions.

Leader can respond to the composite list of questions. There may be a few questions that could be answered directly by the leader. However, his comments may be more appropriate if they include the following:

- *All questions are good questions.*

- *Although we might wish someone would give us all the answers it is important that we work at finding our own answers.*

- *We need to learn how to use some Bible study tools and to discover which tools will help us with particular questions.*

- *After doing some practice with the tools and some research we will return to our list of questions to share some of our discoveries.*

ACTIVITY FOUR: BIBLE CONCORDANCE

Sometimes we have questions about where to find particular Bible passages or we want additional passages on a specific subject. A **Bible Concordance** is a very helpful tool in finding Bible passages.

Each participant, or pair of participants, should have a Concise Bible Concordance in front of him.

Show on a chart or transparency the following definition:

"A CONCORDANCE IS AN ALPHABETICAL LIST OF THE IMPORTANT WORDS IN A BOOK WITH REFERENCES TO THE PASSAGES IN WHICH THEY OCCUR."

Before using a Concordance instruct participants to find the Lord's Prayer in the Bible. (Many persons are not able to find the Lord's Prayer without some help.)

After persons have had difficulty finding the Lord's Prayer the leader can comment:

> *- If we depend just on our memory to find passages in the Bible, we are limited.*

> *- If we depend on flipping through the pages to find a passage, we are also limited.*

> *- To find something specific we need the help of a person who knows where it is, or we need a "tool" like a Concordance.*

Let's use the Concordance. Turn to the word PRAYER. Notice there are lots of verses listed under that word. But, we will not find the Lord's Prayer because that is a title given to a prayer. We need to look under words that are a part of the prayer itself. What are some words that might help us?

The participants may suggest words such as: **Father, Heaven, Hallowed, Kingdom, Earth, Bread, Temptation,** etc. (Using THE RSV HANDY CONCORDANCE from Zondervan persons would have been able to find a verse from the Lord's Prayer under the words **Father, Heaven, Hallowed, Temptation,** and **Trespasses.**)

Following is a re-print of the references listed under the word HEAVEN.

In order to provide opportunity to practice the skill of using the Concordance encourage participants to suggest some verses they recall but do not know where to find in the Bible. After searching for half a dozen verses the skill should be reinforced enough for everyone to feel confident in using a Concordance.

A word of caution: When using a Concise Concordance you will not always find every verse you look for. A Concise Concordance is limited in that it only includes the more familiar passages. However, a Concise Concordance will be sufficient for most students most of the time.

ACTIVITY FIVE: BIBLE CROSS REFERENCE FOOTNOTES

Jesus was asked by someone: "Which is the great commandment in the law?" Jesus' answer was, "You shall love the Lord your God with all your heart, and with all your soul, and with all your mind." (Matthew 22:37)

Find this passage in the Gospel of Matthew using a Concordance.

Leader introduces cross-reference footnotes at the bottom of the page. Notice bold print numbers are the verses in Matthew and the light print text following is where this verse appears in other places in the Bible.

Following is a page from the Revised Standard Version of the Bible.

MATTHEW 22   24   *The Great Commandment*

living." ³³And when the crowd heard it, they were astonished at his teaching.

34 But when the Pharisees heard that he had silenced the Sad'dū·ceeś, they came together. ³⁵And one of them, a lawyer, asked him a question, to test him. ³⁶ "Teacher, which is the great commandment in the law?" ³⁷And he said to him, "You shall love the Lord your God with all your heart, and with all your soul, and with all your mind. ³⁸ This is the great and first commandment. ³⁹And a second is like it, You shall love your neighbor as yourself. ⁴⁰ On these two commandments depend all the law and the prophets."

4I Now while the Pharisees were gathered together, Jesus asked them a question, ⁴² saying, "What do you think of the Christ? Whose son is he?" They said to him, "The son of David." ⁴³ He said to them, "How is it then

and being called rabbi by men. ⁸ But you are not to be called rabbi, for you have one teacher, and you are all brethren. ⁹And call no man your father on earth, for you have one Father, who is in heaven. ¹⁰ Neither be called masters, for you have one master, the Christ. ¹¹ He who is greatest among you shall be your servant; ¹² whoever exalts himself will be humbled, and whoever humbles himself will be exalted.

13 "But woe to you, scribes and Pharisees, hypocrites! because you shut the kingdom of heaven against men; for you neither enter yourselves, nor allow those who would enter to go in.ᵛ ¹⁵ Woe to you, scribes and Pharisees, hypocrites! for you traverse sea and land to make a single proselyte, and when he becomes a proselyte, you make him twice as much a child of hell as yourselves

ᵗ *Or David in the Spirit* ᵘ Other ancient authorities omit *hard to bear*
ᵛ Other authorities add here (or after verse 12) verse 14, *Woe to you, scribes and Pharisees, hypocrites! for you devour widows' houses and for a pretense you make long prayers; therefore you will receive the greater condemnation* ʷ Greek *Gehenna*
22.33: Mt 7.28. 22.34-40: Mk 12.28-34; Lk 20.39-40; 10.25-28. 22.35: Lk 7.30; 11.45; 14.3.
22.37: Deut 6.5. 22.39: Lev 19.18; Mt 19.19; Gal 5.14; Rom 13.9; Jas 2.8.
22.41-46: Mk 12.35-37; Lk 20.41-44. 22.44: Ps 110.1; Acts 2.34-35; Heb 1.13; 10.13.
22.46: Mk 12.34; Lk 20.40. 23.4: Lk 11.46; Acts 15.10.
23.5: Mt 6.1, 5, 16; Ex 13.9; Deut 6.8; Mt 9.20. 23.6-7: Mk 12.38-39; Lk 20.46; 14.7-11; 11.43.
23.8: Jas 3.1. 23.11: Mt 20.26; Mk 9.35; 10.43; Lk 9.48; 22.26.
23.12: Lk 14.11; 18.14; Mt 18.4, 1 Pet 5.6. 23.13: Lk 11.52. 23.15: Acts 2.10; 6.5; 13.43.
23.16-22: Mt 5.33-37; 15.14. 23.17: Ex 30.29. 23.21: 1 Kings 8.13; Ps 26.8.
23.23-24: Lk 11.42; Lev 27.30; Mic 6.8.

Using the footnotes find the Matthew 22:37 verse in the book of Deuteronomy. Then find it in Mark and Luke. Also, find Matthew 22:39 in Leviticus and other places in the New Testament.

Spend a few minutes comparing the same passage in Matthew, Mark, and Luke by answering the following questions.

    a. Who asks Jesus the questions?
    b. Why is Jesus asked the question?
    c. What is Jesus' response to the question?
    d. How does the questioner respond to Jesus?
    e. What else happened?

Notice that there are some differences between the three gospels in terms of some of the details. However, the truth of the message is the same.

ACTIVITY SIX: BIBLE DICTIONARY

Each participant, or pair of participants, should have a copy of a Bible Dictionary to use for the following activities. See page 52 for suggestions of some helpful Bible Dictionaries.

The Bible Dictionary gives more than definitions. Look at the word COVENANT. The paragraph or two includes a description of how the word is used in the Bible, plus some biblical references.

Use the Bible Dictionary to find answers to some of the following questions. Each person, or pair of persons, can choose which questions to answer. Work on as many questions as interest you or as you have time for in the ten minutes we have to work.

SOME QUESTIONS*

a. What is the difference between the two words APOSTLE and DISCIPLE?

b. What is the other name for MT. SINAI? Where is the mountain located?

c. Who was EUTYCHUS? Why is he remembered?

d. What does the name EZEKIEL mean?

e. Who were the SADDUCEES and the PHARISEES?

f. What is a PARABLE?

g. What does the word GOSPEL mean?

---

*These questions are just examples of the types of questions that could be asked. The leader should prepare his/her own list of questions.

After spending ten minutes searching for answers to the questions, persons can share what they have discovered and also share their feelings about the experiences of using Bible Concordances, Footnotes and Dictionaries.

ACTIVITY SEVEN: BIBLE SCAVENGER HUNT

Now that participants in the class have become familiar with some of the basic tools for Bible study it is possible to reinforce those skills and have some fun by playing a Bible Scavenger Hunt.

The leader may desire to reorganize the participants into different groupings. Each group should include five persons. One way to achieve this would be to select the six youngest persons in the class (assuming a class of thirty persons).

Each of these "youngest children" select an older "brother" or "sister". The older "brother" or "sister" choose a "mother" or "father" for their group. The "mother" or "father" chooses another member of the "family".

The "temporary families" will work together on the scavenger hunt. This regrouping gives persons a chance to work with others than those in their own personal family.

Allow twenty minutes for the Scavenger Hunt. Give each participant a worksheet which lists all the items. The leader may want to change, add, or substitute items with those on the worksheet. Use any or all of the tools available for finding information.

After spending twenty minutes searching, announce that "time is up." Check to see which group has the most right answers. Compare all the answers. Be sure each person ends up with a worksheet filled out with all the right answers. Spend some time discussing any questions that arise.

BIBLE SCAVENGER HUNT

1. Find Deuteronomy 6:5. List three places in the New Testament where this verse is quoted.

   _____   _____   _____

2. Find the shortest _____ and the longest _____ psalms.

3. Find two places in the Old Testament where the Ten Commandments are listed...

   _____   _____

4. Name a book in the Bible which represents each of the following kinds of writing.

   Law _____   Prophecy _____

   Poetry _____   Gospel _____

   History _____   Letter _____

5. List the names of all twelve disciples (apostles).

   _____ _____ _____ _____

   _____ _____ _____ _____

   _____ _____ _____ _____

6. Write ten important facts about any person in the Bible.

   _____   _____

   _____   _____

   _____   _____

   _____   _____

   _____   _____

7. State the original occupations of the following Bible persons:

   Moses _____   Jesus _____

   Amos _____   Matthew _____

   Peter _____   Paul _____

8. Determine the approximate mileage between:

   Ur and Haran _____ miles

   Haran and Bethel _____ miles

   Land of Goshen and Mt. Sinai _____ miles

   Nazareth and Bethlehem _____ miles

   Jerusalem and Corinth _____ miles

9. Name six bodies of water mentioned in the Bible

   _____   _____   _____

   _____   _____   _____

10. Place the following events in chronological order:

    _____ Baptism of Jesus

    _____ Call of Abraham

    _____ Preaching of Jeremiah

    _____ Resurrection of Jesus

    _____ Execution of John the Baptist

_____ David Anointed King of Israel

_____ Captivity in Babylon

_____ Day of Pentecost

_____ Creation

_____ Feeding of the 5000

_____ Writing of Gospel of Mark

_____ Captivity in Egypt

_____ Call of Moses

_____ Paul in Rome

Answers for the Scavenger Hunt:

1. Matt. 22:37, Mark 12:30, Luke 10:27

2. Psalms 117 and 119

3. Exodus 20:1-17 and Deut. 5:6-21

4. Law: Numbers and others
   Poetry: Psalms and others
   History: Acts and others
   Prophecy: Isaiah and others
   Gospel: Matthew, Mark, Luke and John
   Letter: Romans and others

5. Peter, Andrew, James the Son of Zebedee, John, Philip, Bartholomew, Thomas, Matthew (or Levi), James Son of Alphaeus, Thaddaeus, Simon the Cananaean, and Judas Iscariot (from Matthew 10:2-4)

6. Check the list of facts with a Bible Dictionary or other resource

7. Moses: Sheepherder
   Amos: Sheepherder and dresser of Sycamore trees
   Peter: Fisherman
   Jesus: Carpenter
   Matthew: Tax Collector
   Paul: Tentmaker

8. Use mileage scale on a map in the atlas to determine your estimates

9. Possible correct answers (and there are others)

Dead Sea	Sea of Galilee	Euphrates River
Jordan River	Red Sea	The Great Sea
Sea of Reeds	Mediterranean Sea	
Nile River	Tigris River	

10. Creation, Call of Abraham, Captivity in Egypt, Call of Moses, David anointed King, Preaching of Jeremiah, Captivity in Babylon, Baptism of Jesus, Execution of John the Baptist, Feeding of 5000, Resurrection of Jesus, Day of Pentecost, Paul in Rome, Writing of Gospel of Mark.

SOURCES OF RESOURCES

In this unit we have emphasized developing skills with basic "tools" for doing Bible study. The following resources are samples of the kinds of books that should be available to a group doing the activities suggested.

1. **BIBLES** - When working with a group on Bible skills it is important that each person have a Bible with which to work. It is very helpful to the leader and participants if everyone has a copy of the same version and edition of the Bible so that page numbers can be used to find places. Also, everyone can follow the instructions of the leader related to footnotes, cross-references, and study helps if they can follow along in the same Bible the leader is using.

When selecting Bibles to recommend one is caught between choosing an inexpensive edition or a more complete and more expensive edition. Cokesbury Book Stores offer several dozen different Bibles. Their most popular classroom and pew Bible sells for between three and four dollars, has 30 pages of study helps, maps, illustrations and chronology of the New Testament. The limitation of this edition is that the print is very small and the cover and binding will not withstand heavy classroom use.

On the other hand Cokesbury offers more complete study Bibles which include brief concordances, study helps, footnotes, maps and either introductions to the books of the Bible or brief dictionaries. These Bibles sell for $8.50 to $13.95 each. When buying a quantity of Bibles I can understand why churches with limited budgets purchase the less expensive Bibles. However, if one looks at a Bible as a long-term investment, whether for an individual or a church, then it seems to me some ways need to be developed to provide the Bibles with more resources and longer lasting value.

Write to your nearest Cokesbury Book Store service center for their latest catalog. If possible it would be better to visit a book store to compare Bibles.

2. **CONCORDANCES** - There are two general types of Concordances. (a) The large, comprehensive Concordance which includes every listing and every word of the Bible and (b) a concise, abridged Concordance which includes the more frequently remembered and referred to passages. For use in classroom activities a concise concordance would be very adequate. As of this writing I know of several concise concordances:

THE OXFORD CONCISE CONCORDANCE, published by Oxford. Hardback, sold for $3.00 to $4.00, compiled by B. Metzger and I. Metzger.

THE RSV HANDY CONCORDANCE*, published by Zondervan. Paperback, sold for about $2.00, includes outline of main events in the lives of key persons.

* Available from Griggs Educational Service

3. **BIBLE DICTIONARIES -** There are many different Bible Dictionaries. Large multi-volume dictionaries are excellent tools for the Bible scholar, but not very practical for church classroom use. In groups with children, youth, and adults it is helpful to have several different Bible dictionaries aimed at different age levels and reading abilities.

HARPER'S BIBLE DICTIONARY by M.S. Miller and J.L. Miller; Harper and Brothers, Publishers, 1954.

THE NEW WESTMINSTER DICTIONARY OF THE BIBLE, edited by H.S. Gehman; The Westminster Press, 1969.

YOUNG READERS DICTIONARY OF THE BIBLE, Abingdon Press 1969.

BIBLE ENCYCLOPEDIA FOR CHILDREN by Cecil Northcott; The Westminster Press 1964.

THE HANDY DICTIONARY OF THE BIBLE* Published by Zondervan Paperback, sold for about $2.00.

4. **BIBLE ATLAS**

THE GOLDEN BIBLE ATLAS   Ideal atlas for children's use. Tells the story of the lands of the Bible from Old and New Testament times to the present in simple, easy-to-read language. Fully illustrated with more than 100 color and black-and-white photographs and illustrations. Approximately $4.00.

OXFORD BIBLE ATLAS Edited by Herbert G. May. This completely up-to-date atlas is printed in full color with a three-dimensional effect on each map. Contains historical maps, vegetation maps, rainfall maps, relief maps, gazetteer, and special articles. Cloth edition about $10.00.

* Available from Griggs Educational Service

UNIT TWO....EXPLORING BIBLE PERSONS

A. INTRODUCTION

After persons have developed some basic Bible study skills it is possible for them to engage in a process of exploring some of the interesting and important information about key persons in the Bible.

It is one thing to **learn about** persons who lived long ago; it is quite a different experience to **identify with** a person of the Bible. The activities in this unit are designed to help persons identify with the circumstances and characteristics of Bible personalities.

This unit of study could involve any number of participants. It is planned for the unit to take two or three sessions of one hour each. By involving a small group of participants in the exploration of two or more Bible persons the unit could be extended to four to five sessions. Also, this unit could be completed in one session of two or three hours.

B. UNIT OBJECTIVES

At the end of this unit persons should be able to:

1. Use Bible resource books to find important information about one person of the Bible.

2. Relate one biblical person to other biblical persons who appear before and after.

3. Identify in a personal way with some of the qualities, characteristics and circumstances of a biblical person.

4. Express in a creative way their interpretation of the importance of a key biblical person.

C. MATERIALS NEEDED

Bibles, Bible Resource Books, paper and pencils. Name tags with names of Bible persons. Slide making materials and slide projector.

D. SEQUENCE OF ACTIVITIES
PREPARATION FOR TEACHING ACTIVITIES

This unit can focus on either Old Testament or New Testament persons. Or, the leader could plan for two sessions on Old Testament persons followed by two sessions on New Testament persons. A fifth session could be planned to present all the visual creations of the participants.

Possible Old Testament Persons

Rebecca	Amos	Josiah	Ezekiel	Gideon
Ezra	Aaron	Saul	Samuel	Jezebel
Jeremiah	David	Miriam	Isaac	Solomon
Joshua	Sarah	Nehemiah	Hosea	Absalom
Jonathan	Deborah	Moses	Joseph	Isaiah
Jacob	Abraham	Rachel	Elijah	Esau

Possible New Testament Persons

Andrew	James (brother of Jesus)	Judas Iscariot
John the Baptist	James (son of Zebedee)	Mary (mother of Jesus)
Mary Magdalene	John Mark	Paul
Matthew	Nicodemus	Thomas
Peter	Silas	Timothy
Titus	Barnabas	Jesus
Luke	Philip (the Apostle)	Stephen

Prepare name tags representing the Bible persons (self adhesive labels work well) for the participants to select and wear for the duration of the class period.

ACTIVITY ONE: SELECT A NAME OF A BIBLE PERSON

All the names of the Bible persons that are to be used should be displayed in some visible way so that participants can see all the names and decide which one to choose.

Each person selects a name and receives the name tag of that Bible person.

ACTIVITY TWO: SEARCH FOR INFORMATION

The following instructions should be printed and visible for all participants to refer to during their searching.

INSTRUCTIONS

Spend about fifteen minutes. Use whatever resources you choose in order to find answers to the following three questions:

1. What are some interesting and important bits of information about your person?

2. Who are some other persons important in your person's life?

3. What is the approximate date when your person lived?

There should be a variety of books and other resources available that will help persons of all ages and levels of reading ability.

After everyone has had about fifteen minutes to work, check to see how they are doing. Encourage everyone to try to find an approximate date for their person so that they will be successful in a later activity. The leader could guide some of the participants directly to a time-line.

ACTIVITY THREE: INTRODUCING THE BIBLE PERSONS IN A TIME—LINE

When everyone has a date and some information they are ready for the next instructions.

> *Everyone write a sentence or two to introduce your person to the others. Write the introduction in the first person as if you are the person telling something about yourself to another person.*

After a few minutes of writing a brief introduction, the participants can be instructed to form themselves in a time-line where the Bible persons are arranged in chronological order. Where there are large gaps of time between one Bible person and another that time can be represented by empty space in the time-line. Each person in turn, starting with the earliest, introduces him/herself in the role of the Bible person. The time-line should be in the shape of a shallow semicircle so that everyone can see the other persons.

At the conclusion of the introductions the leader could guide a brief discussion beginning with questions like:

1. *What are some impressions you have about this whole group of Bible persons?*

2. *What were some things that made these persons special and memorable?*

3. *If you could meet one of these persons which one would you choose to meet? Why?*

ACTIVITY FOUR: CREATIVE EXPRESSION WITH SLIDES AND CAPTIONS

Each participant has some basic information about at least one Bible person. Using that information it is possible to create several slides to communicate something significant about the person. There are three types of do-it-yourself slides suggested: 1) Write-On slides, 2) scratch slides, and 3) picture-lift slides. The leader can use these as suggested or substitute other visual expression materials to accomplish the same objective. The materials suggested may all be available locally, but from several sources.

Each participant can create several slides in one or more of the following formats.

1. Write-On Slides

A Write-On Slide is a piece of matte acetate in a 2″x2″ cardboard frame. Students can use projection pens or pencils to draw and write directly on the slide. The slide is ready for projection immediately. It is possible to draw or write on both sides. (One side is shiny and smooth, the other is dull and textured.) If water soluble projection pens and pencils are used the slides can be washed off with a soft, damp cloth and used again.

2. Scratch Slides

Collect some exposed slides from your photographer friends. Often the end of a slide roll has been mounted so that there are several black, opaque slides. Black sides also result when the shutter is released and the lens cap has not been removed. Photographers usually throw these rejects away. By scratching with a sharp instrument on the side of the slide coated with the emulsion it is possible to scratch off the emulsion leaving a clear, transparent scratch. By scratching carefully beautiful images can be created. These images can be colored with projection pens or pencils to produce a very colorful slide. Push pins, dissecting needles, and other sharp instruments can be used as scratchers.

3. Picture Life Slides

By using Pic-Lift Plastic and Plastic Slide Squares it is possible to use magazine pictures to create transparent slides. The following instructions are guaranteed to produce excellent results. (You can substitute Clear-Contact Plastic for Pic-Lift Plastic and acetate for the Plastic Slide Square. However, you must insert the Contact and Acetate in a Super Slide Mount in order to project in the slide projector. We do not guarantee the results when using Con-Tact Paper.)

1. Find a picture (or other materials) in a magazine which is printed with a clay base on slick paper. Covers do not work well. Some of the magazines appropriate for this

activity are: Newsweek, Time, Sports Illustrated, National Geographic and many others.

2. Remove one piece of Plastic and place it over the selected picture.

3. Rub the Plastic with a brayer, bottom of a spoon or other hard, smooth object. (We have even used the side of a finger nail and achieved excellent results).

4. Tear the picture with Plastic from the magazine.

5. Soak in a bowl of water for approximately one minute.

6. Remove paper from Plastic. Ink will remain on the Plastic.

7. Rinse off the grey, chalky substance from the Plastic. This grey substance is the clay and must be removed for the slide to be transparent.

8. Let the Plastic dry. Do not rub with paper towel as the sticky side of the plastic will pick up the lint.

9. Mount the Plastic on a 2 x 2 inch Plastic Slide Square.

10. Trim any excess Plastic from the slide.

11. Insert slide into projector to see your excellent results.

After participants have created their slides they should write one or two sentences as the "script" for each slide. The leader will collect the slides in the proper sequence for inserting in the slide tray to be projected. As the slides appear on the screen the one who created the slide reads the "script" he wrote for each slide.

A couple of words of caution:

1. The leader should practice each of the three ways to create slides to be sure he/she understands all the steps.

2. Write out the instructions for each slide format so that participants can do it themselves without the leader having to show every step.

3. Allow some time for the participants to practice and fool around with one slide in the format they choose. They will be much more successful in their production if they can practice a little first.

4. Be sure you know how to operate the slide projector, have an extra bulb, and know how to change the bulb.

HAVE A LOT OF FUN!

UNIT III . . . JESUS AND HIS FOLLOWERS

A. INTRODUCTION

This outline was designed for a three to four week unit with parents and children in the same group. The primary strategy for experiencing the material of this unit is the use of LEARNING CENTERS. This is not the place to present all the information necessary to plan for and implement Learning Centers. However, there are several key factors that must be considered when involving a large group in using Learning Centers.

1. There needs to be a wide variety of Centers so that the participants can select something of interest to them and have sufficient space and resources with which to work. A good rule of thumb - approximately one center for each 3 to 5 students.

2. All necessary resources and materials should be present in the Center so that students don't waste time or lose interest.

3. Directions should be visible, brief, clear, and in logical sequence so that most students can do the activities in the Center without having to be directed at each step by someone else.

4. Some Centers should be more complex and challenging so that the older or more skillful participants will find something of interest to them. And other Centers should be more basic and simple so that younger participants will be motivated also.

5. Identify each Center with a sign or symbol that indicates where it is and what its focus is. Students could be given a printed "directory" of Learning Centers identifying them by name, number, and brief description. In this way they will be able to make a quicker, more effective choice.

6. Some students will work in one Center a whole period and others will experience several Centers in the same time. That is okay. If the Centers are set up for three weeks some students will experience all the Centers and others only a few of them. That is okay.

7. In some Centers younger students will need to be helped by older ones and in other Centers the younger students will be able to help the older ones.

   If I were doing the planning, I would not use a unit with Learning Centers as the first experience for an intergenerational group that has not been together before. Leaders and participants will be more successful with Learning Centers if they have had the opportunity to become acquainted through working, playing and worshipping together prior to this unit.

   There are enough Learning Centers outlined that a group of 40 to 50 persons would have enough options to involve them for three to four weeks with the Learning Centers. One of the problems of using Learning Centers is that everyone "does his own thing" so that there is not as much sharing and interacting with the whole group. Perhaps the leader will want to plan for time at the end of each session or even a whole session at the end of the unit where the participants will have the opportunity to share and learn from each other. Displays, presentations, or a program of "show and tell" are all ways that this sharing could be facilitated.

B. UNIT OBJECTIVES

Each Learning Center has one or more objectives associated with it. In this unit you will find the objectives at the beginning of each Learning Center description.

C. MATERIALS NEEDED

Instead of making a list here of all the materials needed we will include a list with each Learning Center appropriate to that Center.

D. DIRECTORY OF LEARNING CENTERS

1. Persons Who Followed Jesus

2. Pic-A-Person

3. Jesus and Stories

4. View a Filmstrip on Peter and Jesus

5. Picturing Jesus

6. Jesus Calls Matthew

7. Scripture Cards and Pictures

8. The Gospel of Mark

9. What Difference Does Jesus Make?

10. The Twelve Disciples Jesus Chose

The format of presentation on each Learning Center includes:

1. Title
2. The Objectives
3. Resources necessary to do the activities in the center.
4. The Directions as they would be written for the students to follow in order to be successful.

1. PERSONS WHO FOLLOWED JESUS

OBJECTIVES:

As a result of participating in this Center persons should be able to:

a. Identify by name and with some pertinent information three persons who followed Jesus.

b. Use successfully several Bible study resources to find answers to key questions.

c. Express in a creative way their learnings or impressions of at least one person who followed Jesus.

RESOURCES:

a. Instruction cards prepared with the five steps printed.

b. Worksheets for each student. (see page 60)

c. Several copies of GOOD NEWS FOR MODERN MAN.

d. Resource books including the following or others that are similar:
- THE RSV HANDY CONCORDANCE
- BIBLE ENCYCLOPEDIA FOR CHILDREN
- PEOPLE OF THE BIBLE

- YOUNG READERS DICTIONARY OF THE BIBLE

- THE HANDY DICTIONARY OF THE BIBLE

e. Creative activity resources including

- Write-On slides

- Magazine pictures, photographs, or slides

- Poetry forms (see page 75)

INSTRUCTIONS: (printed and visible for all participants)

STEP ONE:

Select two or three of the following names. Select any two or three that interest you. These are all persons who were followers of Jesus.

Nicodemus	Zacchaeus	Martha
Bartimaeus	Lazarus	Jairus
Mary Magdelene	A Leper	Paralyzed man
Mary, Martha's Sister		

Write the two or three names on your worksheet.

STEP TWO:

Find a scripture passage that tells about each of the persons you selected.

Use the Index in GOOD NEWS FOR MODERN MAN or THE HANDY RSV CONCORDANCE to help you find the passages.

Read the passages. Notice the four questions on the worksheet. Think about those questions as you read.

STEP THREE:

Look up the two or three names you selected in one or more of the following books: (or, others made available by the planning person)

BIBLE ENCYLOPEDIA FOR CHILDREN
PEOPLE OF THE BIBLE
THE HANDY DICTIONARY OF THE BIBLE
YOUNG READERS DICTIONARY OF THE BIBLE

Read as much as you can find about each person you selected. Keep in mind the four questions on the worksheet.

STEP FOUR:

Answer the following questions about each of the persons you selected:

a. Why did Jesus and the person meet?

b. What happened to the person because of the meeting with Jesus?

c. What feelings do you think the person had toward Jesus?

d. What are some examples of experiences persons have like that today?

Write your answers on your worksheet.

STEP FIVE:

Do **one** creative activity to express your ideas and feelings about one or more of the persons you selected.

   a. Create a series of Write-On slides to illustrate the story in your own way.

   b. Write down a list of questions you would ask if it were possible for you to interview the person.

   d. Create a poem or express your impressions of the person with Jesus. Use one of the poetry forms available or make up your own.

Share what you create with a friend, teacher or someone else in the class.

(SAMPLE WORKSHEET)

	Name 1	Name 2	Name 3
Question 1. Why did Jesus and the person meet?			
Question 2. What happened to the person because of the meeting with Jesus?			
Question 3. What feelings do you think the person had toward Jesus?			
Question 4. What are some examples of things that happen like this today?			

2. PICK — A — PERSON

OBJECTIVES

This Center is similar to the previous one, PERSONS WHO FOLLOWED JESUS. In addition to the ten persons included in that Center the leaders could add the names of some of the more familiar disciples. The uniqueness of this Center is that each participant picks the name of one person to be the focus for the study.

As a result of participating in this Center persons should be able to:

a. Describe some interesting and important facts about one person who followed Jesus.

b. Use successfully several Bible study resources to find answers to key questions.

c. Illustrate in a creative way some of their impressions and insights about the Bible Person.

RESOURCES:

a. Identification and instruction cards for the Bible Persons to be studied. (one card for each person)

b. Resource books

c. Necessary creative activity materials. Leaders will have to gather whatever materials are suggested on the instruction cards.

INSTRUCTIONS:

One large poster should be displayed in the Center with the following instructions:

PICK — A — PERSON
INSTRUCTIONS

1. Pick one card at a time.
2. First, read any scripture passages that are recommended.
3. Answer the questions on the card.
4. Write down the answers in your notebook.
5. For questions where you need more information, use one or more Bible resource books that are available on the bookshelves.
6. Do at least one of the creative activities.
7. When you are finished with it, return the Pick-A-Person card to the pack of cards.
8. Share the results of your work with a teacher, friend, parent or child.

In addition to the general instructions the leaders need to prepare an Identity and Instruction Card for each of the persons to be studied. Outlined below are two sample cards. These are intended as samples only. Create your own questions and creative activities for the persons you want the participants to study.

NICODEMUS

FIRST - Read three passages in the Gospel of John -
John 3:1-17   7:45-52   and   19:38-42

SOME QUESTIONS

1. What kind of person was Nicodemus?

2. How do you think he felt toward Jesus?

3. Why do you suppose Nicodemus came to Jesus?

4. What are some feelings Jesus seems to have had toward Nicodemus?

5. What do you think might have happened to Nicodemus after Jesus was gone?

SOME ACTIVITIES (Select **one**)

1. Write a list of questions to ask Nicodemus in an interview. Have someone else ask **you** the questions as if **you are Nicodemus.** Record the interview.

2. Select a creative painting activity to illustrate the relationship between Jesus and Nicodemus.

3. Dress up as Nicodemus and pose for a Polaroid photograph.

MATTHEW

FIRST - Look up the name Matthew in the INDEX of GOOD NEWS FOR MODERN MAN and/or in the RSV HANDY CONCORDANCE. Read all the suggested references.

SOME QUESTIONS

1. What kind of person was Matthew?

2. Why do you think Jesus wanted Matthew to be one of his disciples?

3. What are some reasons why Matthew would not want to be a disciple? What are some other reasons why he would want to be one?

4. How do you think other persons felt about Matthew being a disciple?

5. What do you suppose are some thoughts you might have had about Matthew if you had been one of Jesus' other disciples?

SOME ACTIVITIES (Select **One**)

1. Write out a brief conversation between two tax collectors talking about Matthew.

2. Create two drawings of Matthew; one as a tax collector, the other as a disciple.

3. Select or create some slides to illustrate some important things about Matthew.

3. JESUS AND STORIES

OBJECTIVES:

As a result of participating in this Center persons should be able to:

    a. Recall several stories about Jesus or stories Jesus told.

    b. Find several of the stories in the Bible.

    c. State several questions about one story.

    d. Communicate in a creative way to share one story with others in the group.

RESOURCES:

    a. A collection of stories about and told by Jesus.
(One good source is the American Bible Society. They distribute about thirty pamphlets - scripture portions - for new readers. Send for GOOD NEWS FOR NEW READERS, American Bible Society, P.O. Box 5656 Grand Central Station, New York, N.Y. 10017)

    b. Several different translations of the New Testament.

    c. Paper and Pencils.

INSTRUCTIONS:

In the envelope are ten stories. Some are stories about Jesus. Others are stories Jesus told.

Read as many of the stories as you want.

Choose one of the stories and do the following:

    a. **Find** the story in the Bible.

    b. **Read** the story in another translation of the Bible.

    c. **Write** down a list of three or more questions that come to your mind when you think about Jesus and the story.

    d. **Share** and **discuss** your questions with a teacher or another student.

    e. **Decide** on a way to illustrate your story to share it with others in the group.

4. VIEW A FILMSTRIP ON PETER AND JESUS

OBJECTIVES:

As a result of participating in the Center persons should be able to:

    a. Describe some of the important impressions persons had of Jesus.

    b. Use the Bible and other resources to find key passages about Jesus and Peter.

    c. Express in a creative way their own personal impressions of Jesus and Peter.

RESOURCES:

a. The filmstrip CHRIST IS RISEN produced by John and Mary Harrell (P.O. Box 9006, Berkeley CA 94709). If this filmstrip is unavailable select another. This filmstrip is a very beautiful and brief expression of the life and ministry of Jesus as seen through the eyes of Peter. The narration is in the words of Peter.

b. Filmstrip projector or viewer, record player and screen.

c. Bibles, resource books, paper and pencil.

d. Cinquain and Diamonte poetry forms (See page 75)

INSTRUCTIONS:

STEP ONE: Use filmstrip viewer and record player. Practice with the equipment first to be sure you can operate it.

STEP TWO: View the filmstrip and listen to the recording CHRIST IS RISEN.

STEP THREE: The story is told from the point of view of Peter. As you view the filmstrip think about all the things you are discovering about Jesus and Peter.

STEP FOUR: After viewing the filmstrip make two lists of statements that complete sentences that begin -

JESUS IS........   PETER IS.....

a.   a.
b.   b.
c.   c.
d.   d.

STEP FIVE: Write a Cinquain **or** Diamonte Poem to express some of your thoughts and feelings about Jesus and/or Peter.

5. PICTURING JESUS

OBJECTIVES:

As a result of participating in this Center persons should be able to:

a. Identify with one or more visual images of Jesus.

b. Tell why they selected one or more pictures of Jesus as the way they "see" Jesus.

c. Express visually their own picture of Jesus.

RESOURCES:

a. A collection of teaching pictures, art reprints and other portraits of Jesus.

b. Tack board, push pins, paper, and felt pens.

c. Materials for drawing and/or painting.

INSTRUCTIONS:

STEP ONE: **Browse** through all the pictures of Jesus looking for the ones you like the best.

STEP TWO: **Compare** the pictures of Jesus that you like in order to **select** one or two pictures that you think show Jesus the best.

STEP THREE: **Mount** the picture you selected on the tack board.

STEP FOUR: **Decide** on a title or a caption to accompany your picture and **write** that title or caption on a card to place next to the picture.

STEP FIVE: **Select** whatever materials you prefer to create your own picture of Jesus.

STEP SIX: **Mount** your picture next to the other one you selected and **write** a different title or caption for your picture or **use** the other title or caption you prepared previously.

6. MATTHEW BECOMES A DISCIPLE

OBJECTIVES

As a result of participating in this Center persons should be able to:

a. State some interesting and important facts about Matthew.

b. Describe some of the conflict Matthew must have encountered and felt personally as a result of becoming a disciple.

c. Respond through a creative media to express some feelings or impressions about Matthew.

RESOURCES:

a. Cassette Tape from the FAITH ALIVE Series produced by Thesis Tapes. P.O. Box 11724 Pittsburgh PA 15228. The episode on Matthew is included in Cassette III - 2, "Jesus Calls the Disciples".

b. Cassette recorder (and a listening center if you have such equipment available)

c. Materials for whatever creative activities are planned.

INSTRUCTIONS:

STEP ONE: Listen to the cassette recording that tells about Jesus calling Matthew to become a disciple.

Listen for answers to four questions:

1. What kind of man was Matthew?

2. Why do you think Jesus wanted Matthew to be a disciple?

3. What reactions did others have to Matthew being chosen as a disciple?

4. What changes did Jesus make in Matthew's life?

STEP TWO: Find and read the story in the Bible where Jesus calls Matthew.

STEP THREE: Complete **one** of the following activities.

    a. Create a set of slides to illustrate the story.

    b. Write a newspaper reporter's account of the event.

    c. Tape record a news report of the event.

STEP FOUR: Share with others what you have created.

7. SCRIPTURE CARDS AND PICTURES

OBJECTIVES:

As a result of participating in this Center persons should be able to:

a. Use visual images of the life and work of Jesus to make a presentation of what they believe is important.

b. Select contemporary visuals to express their ideas and feelings about the life and work of Jesus.

RESOURCES:

a. Pack of 20 scripture cards produced by American Bible Society and available from Griggs Educational Service. Or, leaders can make their own scripture cards by cutting line drawings from GOOD NEWS FOR MODERN MAN and mounting them on 4x6 cards. The scripture text could be printed on the back of each card.

b. A collection of photographs clipped from magazines or a stack of magazines.

c. Paper, pencils, magazines, glue, scissors, and butcher paper.

INSTRUCTIONS:

STEP ONE: **Browse** through the pack of Scripture Cards. Just get acquainted with them and enjoy them.

STEP TWO: **Select** as many cards as you would like. Arrange these selected cards in a sequence that communicates a message about Jesus and his followers.

STEP THREE: **Write** your own captions or titles for the cards you selected.

STEP FOUR: **Select** pictures from the picture collection or from magazines that will illustrate in a contemporary way a similar message as the one you created with the Scripture Cards.

OR

Use one or more Scripture Cards as the central focus for creating a montage of your message. Use magazine pictures and word clippings to create your montage.

8. THE GOSPEL OF MARK

OBJECTIVES:

As a result of participating in this Center persons should be able to:

a. State some important facts about the Gospel of Mark as a whole.

b. Recall a number of the miracles Jesus performed as recorded in the Gospel of Mark.

c. Cite some examples of how Jesus responded to persons and how they reacted to him.

RESOURCES:

a. GOOD NEWS FOR MODERN MAN

b. Bible resource books

c. Copies of "Notes on Gospel of Mark" (This is a one page summary of notes from several sources, prepared by the leaders.)

d. Paper, pencils

e. Cassette tape of Mark, Chaps 1-3 and cassette recorder. (Leader can record the reading ahead of time.)

INSTRUCTIONS:

STEP ONE: Read the "Notes on Gospel of Mark" and do some research in the Bible resource books in order to answer the following questions.

a. Who was the author of the Gospel of Mark?
b. Why was the Gospel of Mark written?
c. What are some important characteristics of the Gospel of Mark?

STEP TWO: Listen to the cassette recording of the first three chapters of the Gospel of Mark. As you are listening make a list of statements that all start with "Jesus is . . . . . ." Stop the recorder each time you have something to write.

STEP THREE: Do **one** of the following activities.

a. Skim through as many chapters of Mark as you can looking for all the names or titles of Jesus. After you have a list, select one name or title to do some further research and then create your own symbol to represent that name or title.

OR

b. Skim through as many chapters of Mark as you can looking for all the miracles performed by Jesus. Make a list of them and answer two questions for as many miracles as possible.

- Why did Jesus perform the miracle?
- What happened after the miracle?

OR

> c. Look for actions of Jesus and reactions of the people to Jesus in the Gospel of Mark. Make two columns:

Jesus acted by . . . .   The people reacted to Jesus by . . . .

9. WHAT DIFFERENCE DOES JESUS MAKE?

OBJECTIVES:

As a result of participating in this Center persons should be able to:

a. Describe the differences between the "before" and "after" circumstances of persons who experienced Jesus personally.

b. Suggest some ways that Jesus can make a difference in persons' lives today.

RESOURCES:

a. Nine specific Scripture Cards which include:

1. Jesus Healing Ten Lepers

2. Jesus Calls Four Fishermen

3. Jesus Join's Zacchaeus for Dinner

4. Jesus Calms a Storm

5. Feeding of 5000

6. Jesus Visits Martha and Mary

7. Jesus Forgives and Heals Man Lowered Through the Roof

8. Jesus Encounters Thomas

9. The Miraculous Conversions of Saul

b. Materials necessary for whatever creative activities are planned by the leader.

INSTRUCTIONS:

STEP ONE: There are nine Scripture Cards. Each one represents an encounter Jesus had with other persons. Look at all the Scripture Cards.

STEP TWO: Choose two or three cards that interest you. Read the scripture on the back of the card. Think about the differences or changes Jesus made in the lives of the persons.

68

STEP THREE: Complete **one** of the following activities:

      a. Write your own "before" and "after" stories of the persons with Jesus.

OR

      b. Draw on paper, slides or transparencies "before" and "after" interpretations of the persons with Jesus.

OR

      c. Conduct an interview with another person taking the roles of a reporter and a person who was helped by Jesus. Talk about the changes that happened in the person's life after he/she met Jesus.

10. THE TWELVE DISCIPLES JESUS CHOSE

OBJECTIVES:

As a result of participating in this Center persons should be able to:

    a. Find at least one place in the New Testament where the twelve disciples are listed.

    b. Identify by name and two facts, six of the twelve disciples.

    c. Given a list of twenty names of New Testament persons, identify all twelve disciples.

    d. State in their own words a definition of disciple.

RESOURCES:

    a. GOOD NEWS FOR MODERN MAN

    b. Bible resource books

    c. A game, puzzle, and test focusing on the twelve disciples

INSTRUCTIONS:

Who Were The Twelve Disciples Jesus Chose?

STEP ONE: Use either of the following two books:
BIBLE ENCYCLOPEDIA FOR CHILDREN
YOUNG READERS DICTIONARY OF THE BIBLE
Look up the word DISCIPLE and read the definition.

STEP TWO: Complete the sentence in your own words—

A disciple is _____

_____

_____

STEP THREE: Find at least one place in the New Testament where the twelve disciples are listed.

Use Bible references in one of the books or index in GOOD NEWS FOR MODERN MAN to find a place where the disciples are listed.

Hint: Look under the word APOSTLE also.

The twelve disciples (apostles) were:

1.	7.
2.	8.
3.	9.
4.	10.
5.	11.
6.	12.

STEP FOUR: To find out more about the disciples or to help you remember their names you can choose to do one of the following fun things.

    a. Finish a Crossword Puzzle

    b. Use the Bible Study-Scope Tube

    c. Play a game of cards - Disciple Rummy

    d. Use the Electric Response Board

SAMPLE ACTIVITIES FOR SOME LEARNING CENTERS

What follows are some examples of games, puzzles and forms that could be used in some of the learning centers. We suggest that leaders use these as samples to give them ideas of some things they can make up to fit their particular situation and not use them directly.

A. CROSSWORD PUZZLES ON THE APOSTLES

1. THE APOSTLES

DOWN

1. Was a tax collector when Jesus called him. (Matthew 9:9)

2. Known as the doubter. (John 20:24-29)

3. Name changed from Simon to _____ which means "rock". (Matthew 16:13-20)

5. The one elected to take Judas' place (Acts 1:21-26)

6. Not one of the original twelve apostles, but identified as an apostle and author of many letters in the New Testament. (Romans 1:1)

11. Known as a zealot. (Matthew 10:4)

14. The one who betrayed Jesus for thirty coins (Matthew 26:14-16)

ACROSS

4. A lesser known apostle, his name means "son of Talmai". (Matthew 10:3)

7. A fisherman from Capernaum and brother of Peter. (Matthew 4:18-20)

8. A lesser known apostle, also called Judas son of James. (Matthew 10:3 and Luke 6:16)

9. The apostle who brought Nathaniel to Jesus. (John 1:43-46)

10. A son of Zebedee. (Matthew 4:21-22)

12. A son of Alphaeus. (Matthew 10:3)

13. A fisherman, one of the inner circle of disciples closest to Jesus. (Matthew 17:1)

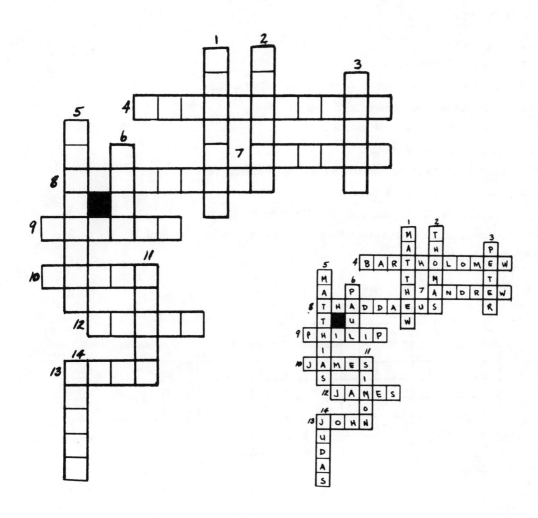

2. PETER, THE APOSTLE

DOWN

1. Peter's work before he became a disciple.

2. When asked at Jesus' trial if he knew Jesus, Peter _____ knowing him.

3. Peter _____ that Jesus was God's Messiah.

5. The garden where Jesus prayed and the disciples slept before Jesus' arrest.

6. On the day of Pentecost Peter _____ to many people.

9. The Greek word meaning "Messiah".

11. The one to whom Peter said, "You are the Christ, the Son of the living God."

13. Peter's brother.

ACROSS

4. A Jewish festival fifty days after Passover.

7. A person who follows and learns from Jesus is called a _____ .

8. In Greek the name Peter means _____ .

10. The city where Peter spent his last days.

12. Peter _____ a lame man.

14. Peter was also called by an Aramaic name which means "rock".

15. Peter's name before Jesus changed it.

16. Peter was an important _____ of the early church.

17. Three _____ (epistles) bear Peter's name in the New Testament.

18. Peter fell when he tried to walk on _____ .

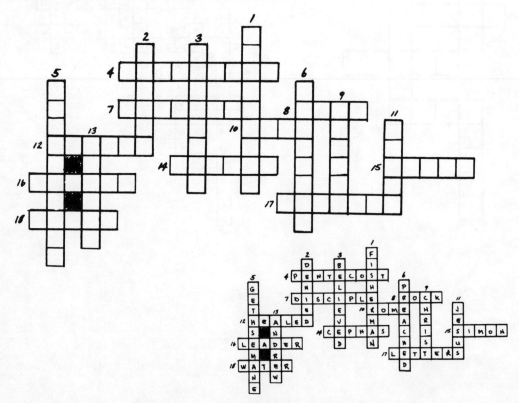

72

B. THREE MATCHING WORKSHEETS

Matching games can be put on ditto sheets, magnetic boards, flannel graph boards, or electric response boards.

Match Column A with the correct answer in Column B.

1. PETER, THE APOSTLE

Column A   Column B

Before being called by Jesus to be a disciple Peter was a _____ .   Pentecost

Peter's brother was _____ .   Simon

When Jesus asked Peter, "Who do you say that I am? Peter answered _____ .   True

Before being named "Peter" by Jesus his name was _____ .   John Mark

The name "Peter" means _____ .

(true or false) Peter was always like a "rock" in his faithfulness to Jesus.   False

A man who was a companion of Peter and author of one of the Gospels.   "You are the Christ, the Son of the living God"

The disciples were gathered in Jerusalem when they received God's Holy Spirit and Peter preached on the day of   Rock

_____ .   Fisherman

The city where Peter was crucified and buried.   Rome

What are some words you could use to describe Peter?   Andrew

2. JESUS' DISCIPLES

Column A	Column B
A fisherman from Capernaum and brother of Peter.	Matthias
The one who betrayed Jesus for 30 coins.	Philip
Was a tax collector when Jesus called him.	
Name changed from Simon to _____ which means "rock."	Matthew
Known as the doubter.	Andrew
The one elected to take Judas' place	
A fisherman, one of the 12 disciples closest to Jesus.	Judas
Not one of the original 12 but identified as an Apostle.	Thomas
The disciple who brought Nathaniel to Jesus.	James
The other son of Zebedee.	John
	Paul
	Peter

3. OTHERS WHO FOLLOWED JESUS

Column A	Column B
A pharisee, asked Jesus good questions. Helped to bury Jesus.	Joseph of Arimathea
A tax collector, a small man Jesus visited in his home.	Lazarus
Jesus talked with this woman at a well about "living water" and "true worship."	Bartimaeus
Brother of Mary and Martha - Jesus brought him back to life.	Jairus
A woman follower of Jesus. Present at his crucifixion and resurrection.	Mary Magdalene
Lived in Bethany. The sister who was busy with housework.	Mary
A synagogue official whose daughter was healed by Jesus.	Zacchaeus
A blind beggar who was healed by Jesus and then became a follower.	Nicodemus
Sister of Lazarus who paid careful attention to Jesus' teaching.	Samaritan Woman
A secret follower of Jesus who provided the tomb for Jesus' burial.	Martha

74

C. THREE CREATIVE POETRY FORMS

CINQUAIN Cinquain is a poetry form that has a very special style that it is named for. The word CINQUAIN refers to the number five. There are five lines in the poem. A Cinquain is usually done with these guidelines.

Line 1 Title (a noun: one word)   ____

Line 2 Describes the title (two words)   ____ ____

Line 3 Action words or phrase about
    the title (three words)   ____ ____ ____

Line 4 Describes a feeling about
    the title (four words)   ____ ____ ____ ____

Line 5 Refers to the title (one word)   ____

DIAMONTE A Diamonte poem uses opposites. First choose a key word. Put it in the first line. Think of an opposite. Put this in the last line. Follow the directions in column A and put your response on the line with the same number in column B. The middle line (7) is a summary line that brings both opposites together.

Column A	Column B
1. Noun	1. _____
2. Noun which is opposite or a contrast to the noun used on line 1.	3. _____ _____
3. Two words that describe the noun on line 1.	5. _____ _____ _____
4. Two words that describe the noun on line 2.	7. _____
5. Three "-in words" that are action words related to the noun on line 1.	6. _____ _____ _____
6. Three "-ing words" that are action words related to the noun on line 2.	4. _____ _____
7. A phrase that unites both the nouns (line 1 and line 2)	2. _____

HAIKU The Haiku is a poetry form that has come to us from Japan. Traditionally Haiku are written about some aspect of the natural world and the seasons of the year. We are using the Haiku form for our purposes, and the experiences and feelings expressed are not limited by specific subject matter.

Haiku consist of three, unrhymed, unmetered lines, with five syllables in the first line, seven in the second, five in the third or seventeen syllables in all.

The Haiku is not expected to make a complete statement. Through its seventeen concentrated syllables, it has the power to evoke associations, images, and feelings in a listener or a reader.

—— —— —— —— ——

—— —— —— —— ——

—— —— —— ——

D. BLANK PLAYING CARDS

Many games can be made up to teach biblical facts by using Blank Playing Cards and permanent ink pens. Both products are available from Griggs Educational Service.

Instructions for a game we made up called DISCIPLE RUMMY follow:

DISCIPLE RUMMY RULES

In the deck of cards are names of Jesus' Disciples **and** names of other persons in the Old and New Testament.

Each name has three cards.

The object of the game is to "meld" as many pairs of cards with the names of the Disciples as possible.

You may meld when you have two cards with the same name on them.

TO PLAY

Deal 7 cards.

Put left over cards in the center of the table face down. This pile becomes the "draw".

Each person has a turn in which he -

    Draws one card from the top of the deck to add to his hand.

    Melds any pairs of names (face up on the table)

    Discards one card face up.

A player may pick up the pile of discarded cards instead of taking a card from the "draw" if he has one card in his hand that matches the top card on the discard pile. If he does this he must meld the top card and he must take all the cards in the discard pile. Melded cards do not count for picking up discard pile.

Meld must be put down only when it is your turn and before you discard.

Once you meld you cannot return the cards to your hand.

The game is over when there are no more cards in the draw pile, **OR** when someone goes out (has no cards left in his hand).

When the game ends count your points:

    5 points for each pair of Disciples
    2 points for each other pair of names

    BONUS of 2 points for each set of three matching cards.

    PENALTY of 2 points for each card left in your hand when the game ends.

UNIT FOUR. . . .FAMILY BIBLE STUDY

A. INTRODUCTION

Three session outlines in this unit were designed for use at the Family Festival 1972 at Estes Park, Colorado, sponsored by the Reformed Church in America. Approximately 750 family units were present. They were organized into family clusters composed of all ages with approximately twenty-five persons per cluster. Each cluster was guided by two co-leaders. There were 111 clusters meeting three mornings for about an hour and a half.

A unique feature, and challenge, of this program was that all groups were meeting outside on the lawns and among the trees. With over one hundred small groups, meeting outside, we were limited to the kinds and quantities of equipment and resources we could use. In order to involve all age groups in creative ways it was important to have **some** resources available. We solved this problem by producing a cassette tape with instructions, scripture readings, songs, and stories. Each leader team brought their own cassette recorder. In addition to the cassette tape for leaders to share with their groups each family was provided with a "creativity sack". (A vinyl sack imprinted with Family Festival logo on one side and a happy face on the other.) Each creativity sack was filled with: piece of burlap, scraps of felt, magazine, scripture cards, construction paper, poetry forms, message notes with envelopes and printed sheets with suggestions for meditation. The leader teams were also provided with some scissors, bottles of glue, pencils, extra paper, magazines and felt.

From reports received from many leaders and participants it seems that most persons enjoyed the Bible study, had positive feelings about doing the study as groups of families, and learned much in the process. There were many other activities during the five day festival that were enriched by the Bible study.

B. UNIT OBJECTIVES

At the end of this unit persons, and their families, will be enabled to:

1. Identify some of the feelings of conflict and celebration experienced in their families.

2. Relate three Bible stories to experiences in their own families.

3. Set some goals to accomplish in their families.

4. Reflect on some of their important family traditions.

5. Respond to the needs of other persons in their families and neighborhoods.

C. MATERIALS NEEDED

The materials needed are identified specifically in each session.

D. SEQUENCE OF ACTIVITIES

FIRST SESSION—CONFLICT

After a time for getting acquainted and setting the stage the group will be ready for the first activity.

ACTIVITY ONE: THE PARABLE OF THE LOST SON

The leader could introduce the parable with something like the following statement:

Jesus told stories to help persons understand some important things about relationships with God and between persons. These stories Jesus told are known as parables. A parable is a way of using common, ordinary things that people know about to help explain some other ideas about God that are harder to understand. Today we are going to focus on a parable Jesus told about a father and two sons. One son stays home and helps his father while the other son takes what belongs to him and goes away to a city where he spends all his money.

Before reading the parable organize the large group into three smaller groups. Each small group will identify with **one** of the main characters in the story. It is best for persons to decide for themselves (even the younger children) which characters will be the focus of their interest. However, it is also important that the three groups are fairly evenly divided. Perhaps some will focus on their "second choice" to help even-up the groups. This dividing of the group can be accomplished with instructions such as:

Each of us is going to hear this parable from the point of view of one of the persons in the story. We are going to try to think and feel like one of the characters. We need some people to be fathers, some others to be sons who stayed home, and others to be sons who went away from home. Choose one you want to be.

After checking to see that everyone has made a choice and to see the "spread" of the choices, give one last instruction before reading the parable.

As you listen to this parable put yourself in the place of the person you chose. Think about all the feelings and thoughts your person might have had.

Read the Parable of the Lost Son (Luke 15:11-32) Someone can read while others listen or the others can follow along in their own Bibles. Or, the reading could be recorded on cassette tape by someone who can be a little more dramatic with the reading. Or, the parable can be presented visually as well as verbally with a filmstrip.

ACTIVITY TWO: MEET IN THREE SMALL GROUPS

The three groups are organized according to the three persons of the parable so that all the fathers will meet together; likewise with the two sons. (If the small groups have eight or more persons in them then divide the groups in half so that they will be smaller). In the small groups make a list of all the feelings and thoughts the person might have had and discuss the reasons for those feelings and thoughts. Allow about seven to ten minutes for this smaller group discussion.

ACTIVITY THREE: FAMILY DISCUSSIONS

Regroup and meet in small "family" groups composed of one or two of each of the three persons. There will be many "family" groups all discussing among themselves simultaneously. Each person will speak to others from the point of view of his person (father, or one of the two sons) focusing on two questions:

1. *How do you feel about yourself and what happened to you?*

2. *How do you feel about the other two persons?*

Persons should **share** their feelings and thoughts as clearly and briefly as possible. And they should **listen** to what others have to share.

ACTIVITY FOUR: LARGE GROUP REFLECTION AND DISCUSSION

The group leader(s) can guide the discussion using some of the following questions as guidelines:

1. *What were some of the conflicts in the story?*

2. *How were the conflicts resolved?*

3. *What are some of the conflicts like these in our own families?*

4. *How can we resolve or learn to live with our conflicts?*

5. *What is the main point or message of the parable?*

6. *What are some things you think Jesus was trying to help us discover about ourselves?*

ACTIVITY FIVE: CREATIVE EXPRESSION

There are a variety of possible activities through which persons can express themselves creatively in order to convey to others their understanding of the parable and its meaning for their lives today. Possible creative activities include:

- Writing a Cinquain Poem
- Writing a Haiku Poem
- Selecting magazine pictures and captions to illustrate feelings of persons in the parable, or perhaps to illustrate a poem they or someone else wrote.
- Making a montage with magazine pictures, ads, and captions.
- Paraphrasing the parable using contemporary language and situations.

After a time for creating be sure to provide a time for persons to share with others what they created.

SECOND SESSION—COVENANT

One of the major contributors to the program of Family Festival 1972 was Dr. Roy Rodgers, a sociologist and Presbyterian layman. In his letter to the planning committee he wrote the following to help us think about the concept of **Covenant.**

"For the family who puts their faith in Christ, we have the concept of covenant. This seems to fit well with the idea of strengthening families. If they can learn to handle conflict, they should be stronger for it. Note - I did not say avoid or resolve or eradicate - I said **handle** conflict. Why covenant? Well, I think that the problem in most families that leads to conflict is the inability to accept others as they are. Parents get hung up over how the kids eat, dress, sleep, take baths, etc. Kids do the same on these or other topics with parents. Husbands and wives have the problem and so do siblings. We keep wanting to make people over in our image. But the concept of covenant says, theologically, we have been accepted as we are by God, the Father, and this has been dramatically demonstrated in the New Covenant in Jesus Christ, the Son. Having been accepted, we are reconciled to God and to our fellow man - including our relatives! A covenant is **not** a contract. Certainly, the New Covenant was not. We don't do anything to be accepted. We simply believe. So, in our family relationships, we try to act in a similar manner. We don't put conditions on our willingness to accept our spouses, siblings, or offspring. If God can accept us, who are we to put conditions on our acceptance of others? Furthermore, in a contract, we can legitimately withdraw from the relationship if the other party or parties fail to fulfill their part of the bargain. In a covenant we maintain the relationship, regardless of what the other party may do. Maybe that's enough to give you the idea. So, how about communion? Well, it should be pretty obvious at this point. The consequence of that kind of acceptance is a relationship that is close - that is a genuine kind of communion."

This session is designed to help persons and families to identify and accept their individual uniqueness and to celebrate their acceptance by God.

After a brief time of opening, introduction, or setting the stage the following activities may be appropriate.

ACTIVITY ONE: LISTEN TO WHOBODY THERE?

WHOBODY THERE? is available in both book and filmstrip formats from Griggs Educational Service, 1731 Barcelona Street, Livermore, CA 94550. Designed to be experienced by adults and children together.

This is a story about "whobodies". "Whobodies" are different from "anybodies". "Anybodies" talk at you and don't listen to you, "whobodies" care about you and really listen.

The leader can read the story while everyone listens, or, slides of the photographs in the story can be prepared ahead of time so that persons can see the photos while the story is being read. Or, the story can be recorded by someone with a strong, dramatic voice so that all can listen to the story.

No matter how the story is presented all participants should listen for all the differences between "anybodies" and "whobodies".

ACTIVITY TWO: MAKE LISTS OF WHOBODIES AND ANYBODIES

After listening to the story persons can work in small groups (or family groups) to make two lists in response to the incomplete sentences:

"Anybodies are persons who..........."
"Whobodies are persons who........."

When the small groups have spent a few minutes forming their lists they could share their lists with each other. A composite list could be written on a large sheet of butcher paper.

In response to the composite list that represents contributions from all the small groups, the leader could guide a brief discussion using questions such as:

- *What are some ways we can be "whobodies?"*
- *Are there any times when it is best to be an "anybody?" Give some examples.*
- *What do you think is the main difference between "anybodies" and "whobodies?"*
- *What are some things to do that might help "anybodies" become "whobodies?"*

ACTIVITY THREE: SHARING FAMILY TRADITIONS

There needs to be a transition from the story about whobodies to the focus on family traditions. The transition may include some of the following statements:

We are all whobodies to each other in our families and in this group. One of the things that makes a family very special for everyone in the family is the traditions that families create and celebrate. Families develop traditions around meals, holidays, birthdays, vacations, games, and many other family events. Let's think about and share some of our family traditions.

Each family spend time discussing among themselves some of their traditions. Each person in the family can share one or more of their favorite family traditions. After some time of sharing within the family they should select one or two very special traditions to share with others in the larger group.

During the time for the large group sharing, each family can take a few minutes to share their traditions and to respond to each other.

ACTIVITY FOUR: FOCUS ON ZACCHAEUS

Another transition is necessary between family traditions and the next activity which focuses on Zacchaeus. Some points to emphasize could be:

> We have talked about "Whobodies" and family traditions. These are the kinds of relationships and experiences that make life very special and in many ways, very Christian. Now we want to think about Jesus and some of the relationships and experiences that made him very special to other persons. Zaachaeus was an anybody who became a whobody because of his encounter with Jesus. Jesus' disciples became very special "whobodies" as a result of their experiences with him.

Work in small groups.

Read two different passages of scripture.

> Luke 19:1-10 Jesus' encounter with Zacchaeus.
> Luke 22:7-20 Jesus and his disciples last supper.

After reading the two passages compare them and spend some time discussing questions such as:

> - What are some examples of anybodies and whobodies in these two stories?
>
> - What similarities are there between the meal with Zacchaeus and the meal with the disciples?
>
> - How do we usually go about deciding who is to be invited to a special meal or to whose home we want to go for a special meal?
>
> - Why do you think Jesus decided to go to Zacchaeus' home? Why did he decide to have a last supper with his disciples?

ACTIVITY FIVE: TIME FOR MEDITATION AND CREATIVITY

Encourage each person to spend some time alone or, with another member of his family or a friend, to spend some time in meditation which can be guided by the thoughts that are included on the page, "Something to Think About." Be sure each person has a copy of this page.

While persons are reading, thinking, and praying, it may be appropriate to have some music playing in the background.

After a time of meditation and reflection, encourage persons to create poems, banners, posters, or collages to express some of their thoughts.

"We do not come to believe in
ourselves until someone reveals
that deep inside us something
is valuable....
worth listening to....
worthy of our trust....
sacred to our touch...."

*"AND GOD BREATHED INTO MAN THE BREATH
OF LIFE AND MAN BECAME A LIVING SOUL....A
LIVING BEING.....A LIVING PERSON..."*

WE MUST LEARN TO
CELEBRATE LIFE
WHERE WE FIND IT!

T
O
D
A
Y

IS

*GOD is
AS CLOSE to
us as WE CAN
RISK being
close TO OUR
real selves.*

L O V E P E O P L E
U S E T H I N G S...

SPIRIT
COMES ALIVE
WHEN
WE ARE MADE ALIVE
BY LOVE
SPIRIT EBBS AWAY
WITH LOVE'S DECLINE

LOVE IS....

T
H
E

F
I
R
S
T

D
A
Y

of

*JESUS SAID:
"HURRY DOWN ZACCHAEUS, BECAUSE I
MUST STAY IN YOUR HOUSE TODAY!"*

OUR LIVES ARE SHAPED
BY THOSE WE LOVE
AND THOSE WHO LOVE US.

A PERSON IS CONSTANTLY
CALLED UPON
TO CREATE HIS OWN FUTURE

jesus said:
"i have wanted so
much to eat this passover meal with
you before i suffer."

*"No one has ever seen
God: If we love one
another, God lives in us and his love is made perfect within us.
God is love, and whoever lives in love lives in God and God lives in him"*
(I John 4:12,16)

Believing enough in ourselves to celebrate
GOD - WITH - US
believing enough to say YES
to becoming more a person.

T
H
E

R
E
S
T

of

Y
O
U
R

L
I
F
E

some suggestions.....

1. Spend some time reading, thinking, reflecting on the
    above statements.
2. Choose a way to express some of your feelings and ideas.
    You can do any of the following:
    - write a poem
    - decide on a word, phrase, and/or design from which to
      create a banner
    - make a poster
3. The materials could express your responses to one of the
    following:

I am a person who....   Jesus is special because....
I believe.....   Me and my friends.....
Me and my family.....   I want to be a person who....

THIRD SESSION—COMMITMENT

FIRST ACTIVITY: THE STORY OF WALTER FISH

Walter Fish is a very brief story about a fish who needs help but is ridiculed and ignored. It is a contemporary story that is similar to Jesus' parable of the Good Samaritan. WALTER FISH is available from Alba House Communications, Canfield, Ohio 44406. The story is also available in filmstrip and 16mm film formats.

After listening to the story, the participants can be guided in a brief discussion using questions such as:

Who do you think Walter Fish represents in our world?

Who are some persons or groups that the other characters in the story represent?

What were some problems with the people who encountered Walter Fish?

SECOND ACTIVITY: THE STORY OF THE GOOD SAMARITAN

Before reading or listening have persons keep in mind that this parable which Jesus tells has some things in it that are different and some other things that are similar to the WALTER FISH story.

Read or present the parable of the Good Samaritan by someone reading for the whole group, by having persons read it for themselves, or by using a filmstrip.

After presenting the parable some questions could guide a discussion.

Who were the Priest, the Levite and the Samaritan?

Why do you think Jesus told this story?

What is the main point of the story?

What are the similarities and differences between the stories of Walter Fish and the Good Samaritan?

What are some situations you have heard about or some experiences you have had that are like those two stories?

THIRD ACTIVITY: FAMILIES RESPOND TO NEIGHBORS

Persons will work in family groups to make lists of persons they know in their own families or communities who need neighbors, friends, and the love and concern of others.

After a few minutes of working on their lists the families can share some of the persons on their lists by telling a little about the ones they mention.

The leader can guide the whole group in a brief discussion of some ways it would be possible to be Jesus' kind of neighbor to these persons.

Each family, or member of the family, can decide on one person to whom to respond with some actions of caring and love. Decisions should be made regarding specific ways they are going to relate to the persons they have identified as needing the response of a caring neighbor. There are many possible actions which may include:

- A phone call or note

- An invitation for a meal

- Providing transportation

- A visit for conversation

- Helping accomplish some task the persons are unable to do for themselves.

FOURTH ACTIVITY: RESPONDING WITH CREATIVITY

Individuals, small groups or families could spend the remaining time of the session responding to the theme of the session with some special creativity. Possible activities include:

a. Use magazine pictures to illustrate the Parable of the Good Samaritan.

b. Writing a paraphrase of the parable with familiar contemporary words and examples.

c. Use note cards to write to persons in the family or community who need to hear from a friend and neighbor.

d. Create a banner or sign to proclaim a message of love and concern for other persons.

e. Any other creative activities that the leaders plan for.

After spending time creating it is important for persons to have a chance to share what they have created.

The Session could be concluded by everyone standing in a circle, holding hands, and singing "They'll Know We are Christians By Our Love."

UNIT FIVE. . . .CREATION AND CREATIVITY

A. INTRODUCTION

The sessions included in this unit could be rearranged in a variety of ways. The sessions could be used as single experiences without any connection to each other. The sessions could be developed all together through the use of learning centers. Single sessions from this unit could be added to other units. Or, the four sessions could be presented together in a sequence of four weeks.

B. UNIT OBJECTIVES

Each session has specific objectives which are stated as a part of the session. In addition the following are some objectives that may be accomplished as a result of experiencing the whole unit.

At the end of this unit participants should be able to:

1. Express their own concepts of God's work as creator.

2. Describe ways that they are participants in and benefactors of God's creative work in the world.

C. MATERIALS NEEDED

The following materials will be needed for two or more of the sessions:

1. Bibles and/or GOOD NEWS FOR MODERN MAN

2. Concise Bible Concordances

3. Paper, pencils, felt tip markers

4. Creative Activity Materials

D. SEQUENCE OF SESSIONS AND ACTIVITIES

FIRST SESSION - PSALM 95 and HANDS*

INTRODUCTION

In teaching this session it is important for teachers to have rehearsed in their minds all of the procedures of the session. There are a variety of teaching activities and resources recommended. The pace of the session moves quickly and the teacher needs to be prepared for spontaneous responses, questions, and suggestions which may arise from the students.

OBJECTIVES

At the end of the session the participants should be able to:

1. State their understanding of the Psalmist's concept of God and his meaning of the word "Hand" in Psalm 95.

2. See and feel the importance, power, and creativity of their own hands.

3. Express creatively their individual responses to Psalm 95:1-7 and God's Trombones.

*From 20 NEW WAYS OF TEACHING THE BIBLE by Donald Griggs.

Room Arrangement and Teacher Preparation

It would be helpful to divide the room into two parts. For the biblical study, discussion and listening, place the chairs in a circle. Have one Bible per chair. Place a screen or bulletin board so that it can be seen by everyone. Also, place the phonograph so that it can be reached easily by the leader and heard by the whole class. In the other part of the room (either around the perimeter of the circle or in the other half of the room) have tables (one for each six persons) covered with newspaper or butcher paper. It is best to have chunks of clay already available at the places around the table. Also, provide a dishpan of water and paper towels. It is much more satisfactory to use moist potter's clay available in red, grey or tan from most art supply stores. Plan for about one to two pounds per student.

ACTIVITY ONE. . . .DISCUSSION

Have the students discuss in **pairs** the following assignment.

> *Everybody has some used-to-thinks. Used-to-thinks are those things you used to think and now don't think any more. We are going to discuss some of our used-to-thinks about God. Share with each other some of the things you used to think about God and don't think in the same way any more.*

Allow about five minutes for this.

ACTIVITY TWO. . . .READ AND DISCUSS PSALM 95

Have the class work in **groups of four to six persons** to do the following:

a. Read Psalm 95:1-7

b. Discuss two questions:

1. *What is the writer's idea, image, or concept of God?*
   What does he think God is like?

2. *What is the significance or meaning of the words "hand" and "hands"?*

Allow five to eight minutes for this, then provide an opportunity for the small groups to share with the whole class some of their ideas.

ACTIVITY THREE. . . .FOCUS ON HANDS

There are many ways to focus on Hands. The teacher's own creativity, available resources, and time will determine what is possible.

Some suggestions are: (Don't try to do them all. Try your own approach)

A. Have everyone look at his/her own hands then respond spontaneously as a group to the following questions:

1. What are some things that are important or fun that you do with your hands?
2. What would it be like to be without hands?
3. Why do you think the Psalmist use the word "hands" as a key part of this Psalm?

B. Do some non-verbal creative expression with hands by encouraging persons to communicate feelings of the following:

1. Show anger or frustration

2. Show sadness or loneliness

3. Express friendship to another person

4. Communicate happiness or joy with hands

5. Show you need someone else's help

6. Play a game with another person using hands

7. Shake hands with several people showing them you are glad to see them.

C. Look through magazines to find pictures of hands expressing feelings and actions of hands. Make individual or group montages.

D. Mount several significant pictures or photographs on the tack-board to use as illustrations of feelings that are expressed with hands.

E. Use a print of Michelangelo's painting CREATION OF ADAM showing the creation of man where the hands of God and man are outstretched toward each other. Prepare ahead of time a mask to cover over the whole painting except for a small square which reveals both hands.

ACTIVITY FOUR. . . .SING TOGETHER

Have the group stand in a circle holding hands.

The leader could ask for students to report how they feel as a group now in a circle holding hands compared to when they first came into the room. Or, the leader could express some of his/her own feelings then ask for some responses.

After a minute or two ask if anyone thought of the song "He's Got The Whole World In His Hands." Sing the song encouraging students to suggest words to create new verses to the song. Suggest clapping hands to keep the rhythm.

With the group in a circle holding hands or possibly putting hands and arms around each other's shoulders or waists the feeling of closeness is communicated. Our hands bring us closer to each other. This then would be a natural time for prayer to express thanksgiving for hands and commitment to use our hands for continuing God's creation.

ACTIVITY FIVE. . . .SHARE A POEM

Encourage group to sit down. Allow a minute or two for brief, spontaneous conversation in small or larger groups.

Then describe what is to follow.

1. *We are going to listen to a poem*

2. *After hearing the poem we are going to go to a table where there is clay*

3. *Play and create with the clay in any way that expresses your feelings in response to what we have done or to the poem you will hear.*

(These instructions are helpful **before** the poem so as to avoid having to give any instructions between the hearing of the poem and the moving to work with the clay. Instructions at that point would be an interruption of the thinking and creating process.)

Read the poem from the book *"I'll Make Me A World"*—James Weldon Johnson's Story of the Creation, Viking Press, 1955 and Hallmark Cards, 1972. The poem is also available in the filmstrip titled CREATION produced by Broadman Films, Nashville, Tennessee.

Encourage the students to listen for all the times when hands or arms are mentioned and what actions they perform.

ACTIVITY SIX. . . .CREATE WITH CLAY

Everyone spends 15-25 minutes creating and playing with the clay. Teachers could participate also. Conversation will most likely be informal.

After time for creating, persons can circulate to see what others have done.

The leader may want to "wrap-up" the session by asking the students to reflect upon the day's experience.

> How did it feel to use hands to communicate and create? What was learned about Psalm 95?

Spend a few minutes sharing with each other the products of creating with the clay. Even if a person doesn't have anything to "show" he/she could share some feelings about working with the clay.

SECOND SESSION. . . .EXPERIENCE WITH LIGHT

OBJECTIVES

At the end of the session the participants should be able to:

1. Locate some passages in the Bible that emphasize the concept of light.

2. State in their own words the importance of light.

3. Illustrate in a creative way a Bible passage that focuses on light.

4. Make a connection between the physical reality of light in the world and the symbolic meaning of light as used by Jesus.

MATERIALS NEEDED

Candles and matches, blindfolds, flashlight.

Materials for experimenting with light.

Creative activity materials.

Overhead projector and/or slide projector if needed.

ACTIVITY ONE. . . .RECALL EXPERIENCES WITH LIGHT

The group can start all together, or in small groups (not necessarily family groups), by having each person share any experiences he/she can recall where light was of significance. (Sunburn, lost in the dark, lights, candles etc.)

ACTIVITY TWO. . . .LIGHT IN THE BIBLE

The leader could make a transition from personal experiences involving light to a Biblical focus on light by including some of the following ideas:

> Light is important. We have no life without light. In the creation story we read, "And God said, 'Let there be light', and there was light, and God saw that the light was good."

Jesus said, "I am the light of the world. He who follows me will not walk in darkness but will have the light of life."

It is also true, we have no life without THE LIGHT. We are going to find out more about the place of light in the Bible.

It would be possible for the leader to locate some key passages from Old and New Testaments which emphasize light. Participants could then select which passages to read and discuss. Or, participants could use THE RSV HANDY CONCORDANCE to find their own passages to study and discuss. There are about 55 references to "light" in this particular Concordance. Or, the leader could plan for a combination of the above two activities.

Some questions to think about when reading the Bible passages, and to discuss later, could include:

- *Does the reference to light imply a physical reality or a symbolic meaning?*

- *What is the meaning of light in the passage?*

- *What are some characteristics of light?*

- *What are the sources and uses of light?*

ACTIVITY THREE. . . .THREE ALTERNATIVE ACTIVITIES

Select one of the following activities or proceed to Activity Four if you prefer.

1. View the film PHOS that features the concept of LIGHT. PHOS is a TeleKETICS Film from Franciscan Communication Center.

   "Phos" is the Greek word for light. The film features a Greek Orthodox rite of light on Easter eve.

2. Ask a school teacher or other person who has experience with and interest in some aspects of light who could guide the group in some experiences of or experiments with light. Use lenses or prisms. View through a telescope. Use light sensitive paper or film with which to create.

3. Invite a blind person as a guest with whom the group could discuss his/her concept and experience of light. In what way is the reality and/or symbolism of light important to a person who is blind?

ACTIVITY FOUR. . . .BLINDFOLDED TRUST WALK

Have students choose a partner whom they trust. Give one blindfold to each pair. Spend 30 minutes or so letting the pairs take each other on trust walks. This is especially effective if done someplace other than the classroom. A playground is a good place. Thirty minutes may not be enough time if the students really get involved. If you want to extend the time add a meal to the experience. Eating with a blindfold on really makes us aware of how much we depend upon and take for granted our ability to see.

When you return to the room discuss the experience. How did you feel about not being able to see? About the person who was leading you? About leading the other person?

ACTIVITY FIVE. . . .CELEBRATE LIGHT

Darken the room or go to a room that can be darkened. Sit silently in the dark. Spend a few moments thinking about all the previous experiences of light and dark.

Leader lights one candle and reads from the Gospel of John where Jesus says "I am the light of the world. Whoever follows me will have the light of life and will never walk in darkness."

Allow a few moments of meditation and reflection.

Without a word spoken the leader can direct a flashlight to some pictures mounted on the wall or to some important objects in the room.

If each person has a candle the leader can quote from Matthew 5:14-6 where Jesus said, "You are the light of the world. . . ." while he/she lights his/her own candle and then passes the light on to others so they can light their candles.

While everyone holds his lighted candle a hymn can be sung and a prayer or prayers spoken to conclude the Celebration of Light.

RESOURCE

An excellent resource is:

> LIGHT: A LANGUAGE OF CELEBRATION by Kent Schneider and Sister Adelaide. Published by and available from: The Center for Contemporary Celebration, 1400 E 53rd Street, Chicago Ill 60615

Seldom does one find a book that presents the rationale for the main ideas so that everyone can "tune-in" and at the same time offers very practical, you-can-do-it yourself suggestions to implement the main ideas. In this book the main ideas are Light, Celebration, Media, Persons, Communications, and God.

The book begins: "To search into the meaning of Light is to delve into mystery. . .you will know the LIGHT to the degree you participate in it. . .LIGHT can be shared, yet never diminished; cherished, but never entirely contained; reflected, absorbed, yet, in itself, remains the same."

The book consists of 144 pages organized into six chapters: Knowing Celebration, Total Environment, Overhead Projector, Slide and Film Projection, The Mix of Media, and Designing Celebration. Each chapter contains many photographs and diagrams to help interpret the ideas and techniques that are presented.

Many churches offer contemporary worship services where it is possible to experiment and use a variety of media and materials to enhance the worship experience. This book will serve as an invaluable guide to such churches who seek new resources.

THIRD SESSION. . . .EXPERIENCES WITH COLOR

OBJECTIVES

At the end of the session the participants should be able to:

a. Identify some associations of meaning or experience with a variety of colors.

b. Use colors in creative ways to express feelings messages or a story.

MATERIALS NEEDED

Books about color or which use a lot of colors, and Bibles
Finger paints and paper
Crayons and/or colored chalks and paper
Tape recorder or record player
Overhead projector, clock crystal, food coloring, oil and water
Kaleidoscope and cellophane.

A FEW WORDS ABOUT COLOR

We live in a world of colors. Colors surround us in colorful clothes, color television, colors by the dozens. Colors communicate feelings. Persons respond to colors in various ways. Colors are used as symbols on church vestments. Part of the process of communicating is to learn how to use and respond to colors. There are many ways that emphasis on color can enhance some teaching activities in the church. In this session we plan for persons to become more sensitive and aware of colors as part of God's great creation.

ACTIVITY ONE. . . .INTRODUCTION OF COLOR

Talk about favorite colors. Why is one color a favorite? This sharing could be done in the large group, by family groups, or in other small groups of three or four persons.

Guide persons who select the same color as their favorite to find each other and share their reasons for choosing that color.

Introduce the variety of resources that are available on the tables in the room to experiment with and experience colors.

ACTIVITY TWO. . . .EXPERIENCES OF COLOR

Part of the room can be set up with the following tables of resources. Persons can move from table to table to browse and then select one or two tables to spend more time.

TABLE A	Kaleidoscopes, cellophane, colored plastic pieces and other materials to use to experiment with color. Some Kaleidoscopes have clear glass which can be used to look at persons, pictures, and objects. The resulting images are exciting and beautiful.
TABLE B	Books about color and other books that are colorful. Some books which could be included are: HAILSTONES AND HALIBUT BONES, Mary O'Neill, Doubleday & Company, Inc. THE FESTIVAL OF ART, Gerard A. Pottebaum, Augsburg Publishing House THANK GOD FOR CIRCLES, Joanne Marxhausen, Augsburg Publishing House 3 IN 1 (A Picture of God), Joanne Marxhausen, Augsburg Publishing House 99 PLUS ONE, Gerard A. Pottebaum, Augsburg Publishing House
TABLE C	Record player or tape recorder with music that would be appropriate as background and to motive persons to respond to the music with finger painting.

TABLE D   A listening center with tape recorder where persons listen to a recording prepared by the teacher that would guide the participants to respond with colors. For example, the tape might include:

- Short selections of various kinds of music (loud, soft, fast, slow, dreamy, marching, eerie, joyful, sad etc.)

- Words such as - party, death, fire, lost, children, picnic, cold, wet, gentle, fight, soft, hard etc.

- Sounds such as: door slam, footsteps, crying, laughter, water running, rain storm with thunder, siren, etc.

Instructions on the tape would lead persons to listen and respond to what they hear with colors. Several pieces of paper should be available and a large variety of colors of crayons or chalk.

TABLE E   An overhead projector can be used to create a montage of color. Use a shallow, clear bowl or if you can secure one, a large clock crystal (the glass face of a clock like those in schools and offices. If you want to purchase a clock crystal it can be ordered from Edmund Scientific (801 Edscorp Bldg. Barrington, N.J. 08007.)

1. Place bowl or clock crystal on top of overhead projector.

2. Pour enough water to cover bottom of the bowl.

3. Pour into water some mineral oil. Let the oil appear in a number of globules.

4. Squirt a few drops of food color into the oil. Watch what happens and enjoy the colorful display. Add another color, then another. Rock the crystal gently to see what happens.

ANOTHER WAY TO USE THE SAME MATERIALS

1. Use **two** clock crystals or bowls of the same size.

2. Pour a **little** water in the bottom crystal, add some mineral oil, and one color of food coloring.

3. Place the second crystal inside the first and add some water, mineral oil, and a second color of food coloring.

4. By squeezing the two crystals together you are able to produce an amazing display of designs and color.

5. With a little practice it is possible to move the crystals and colors to accompany music in a way that interprets the music.

TABLE F   With a slide projector and some basic materials to work with, persons could create some beautiful expressions of color. One or more of the following types of slides could be used:

1. Write-On Slides

2. Opaque film scratch slides

3. Picture-Lift Slides

4. Polarized slides

ACTIVITY THREE. . . .SHARING OUR CREATIONS OF COLOR

In family or other small groups or in the whole group or in combinations of small groups persons can share what they have experienced and created. They can discuss whether or not they used their favorite colors, whether they discovered anything about colors, and whether they have any additional favorite colors.

ACTIVITY FOUR. . . .CELEBRATING COLOR

One or more of the following activities could be used to celebrate our experiences of color.

A. Search for one or more Bible verses that would be expressive of one's favorite color.

B. Obtain the film HAILSTONES AND HALIBUT BONES (from Mass Media, 2116 N. Charles Street, Baltimore, Md. 21218) This film expresses in a beautiful, worshipful way the meanings of color.

C. Select some songs and/or hymns that are expressive of color to sing or to listen.

D. Use the story by Mavis Uthe, A STORY ABOUT JESUS, which is written in a very simple language and illustrated with color. This story and directions for how to prepare the colors are presented in the book TEACHING AND CELEBRATING LENT—EASTER by Donald and Patricia Griggs and available from Griggs Educational Service.

E. The Arch Book THE WORLD GOD MADE is now available in filmstrip format from Concordia Publishing House.

This story is presented in outstanding color and sound. With its focus on creation this would be a good way to tie the theme of the whole unit to this particular session.

F. Prayers of thanksgiving for God's gift of colors.

FOURTH SESSION. . . .EXPERIENCES WITH WATER

OBJECTIVES

At the end of the session the participants should be able to:

a. List some ways that water is important to our lives.

b. Find some passages in the Bible that emphasize both the physical reality and symbolic significance of water.

c. Express in a creative way the meaning and importance of water.

MATERIALS NEEDED

Bibles, Concordances, paper and pencils
Film: LET THE RAIN SETTLE IT from TeleKETICS FILMS 1299 South Santee Street Los Angeles CA 90015. 10 minutes, color. $15.00 rental.
Glass pitcher, glasses, water.
Creative activity materials.

ACTIVITY ONE. . . .MEMORIES OF WATER

Divide group into small groups of three to four persons to share their responses to two questions:

> 1. *What are one or two memories you have of experiences that involved water in some way?*
>
> 2. *What feelings do you recall having in relation to those experiences?*

ACTIVITY TWO. . . .A FILM: LET THE RAIN SETTLE IT

Before showing the film, LET THE RAIN SETTLE IT, instruct persons to look for all the places where water appears in any form in the film.

Show the film.

After viewing the film make a list of all the places where water appeared in the film. (Don't miss the tears on the boy's cheeks.)

Discuss what feelings persons associate with each of the examples of water from the film.

In the discussion spend a few minutes comparing the experiences and feelings in the film with the personal experiences and feelings that were identified in the first activity.

ACTIVITY THREE. . . .WATER IN THE BIBLE

Give each person a Bible, or GOOD NEWS FOR MODERN MAN if you want to focus on New Testament. Have some Concise Concordances available, and perhaps a few Bible Dictionaries, so that participants will have some resources available to find passages where water is the central concept.

Each person or small group, is to select one or two passages where water is the central concept. Then, answer two questions related to the passage(s).

> 1. *If water, in this passage, is a physical reality does it have any other symbolic meaning?*
>
> 2. *If water is used symbolically what is its meaning?*

It is helpful in mixed groups for persons to work in twos and threes so that non-readers or beginning readers will have persons who can help them. Each group can share with another group the passage(s) they found and their answers to the questions.

The leader can summarize the focus on water from the Bible by emphasizing the symbol of water used in the Sacrament of Baptism.

ACTIVITY FOUR. . . .TIME FOR CREATING

There is a wide variety of activities that could be planned for the participants to express themselves creatively. The leaders may want to plan for some of the creative activities that were used in previous sessions. If you want additional suggestions of creative activities with complete directions to guide the participants obtain INSTRUCTION CARDS FOR STUDENT CREATIVITY by Patricia Griggs. (Order from Griggs Educational Service)

ACTIVITY FIVE. . . .CELEBRATE WATER

Share the creative expressions of all the participants.

Read one or more of the passages of scripture on water.

Sing a song. One of the most appropriate songs would be PASSED THRU THE WATERS by Avery and Marsh. This song is found in ALIVE AND SINGING, a song book from Proclamation Productions Inc., Port Jarvis, N.Y. 12771.

Use a large glass pitcher filled with cold, fresh water. Give each person a small glass. Move among the persons pouring water in each glass saying the words, "Jesus said, 'You shall never thirst'."

Close with prayer.

UNIT SIX. . . .LET US BREAK BREAD TOGETHER

A. INTRODUCTION

Through the three sessions of this unit we are trying to bring together three different emphases all focused on meals, food or bread: meals we share, the Sacrament of Holy Communion, and world hunger.

Sharing meals is one experience all person in our groups have in common with each other; so we start by focusing on meals. Relationships that are shared with a meal are special relationships. Therefore, we want to spend time focusing on meals that persons shared with Jesus to see if we can discover something about Jesus and his relationships with others. The climax of our study of meals with Jesus will lead us further to think about a special meal Jesus shared with his faithful followers, and which we continue to celebrate in the Sacrament of Holy Communion. After considering breaking bread at meals with others and a Special Meal with Jesus we realize that there are many in the world who do not have bread to eat or to share. Often these same persons are not aware of Jesus as the One who said, "I am the Bread of Life."

This unit could be used in part to focus on Holy Communion in preparation for a celebration of the Sacrament. Or, the Unit could be expanded, especially the part on world hunger, to be co-ordinated with a larger, special program in the church that seeks to involve persons in a program of study and action related to world hunger.

B. UNIT OBJECTIVES

As a result of participating in this unit persons should be able to:

1. Identify some memories and feelings they have that are associated with meals they have shared with other persons.

2. Participate in the planning, preparing, serving and cleaning up of a special meal.

3. Recall some special meals other persons shared with Jesus and describe something of the importance of two or more of those meals.

4. Explain in their own words why the Sacrament of Holy Communion is a very important celebration in the life of the church.

5. Compare some of the parts of the Communion Service with their experiences of relationships with persons and with meals.

6. Identify some of the causes of, examples, and possible solutions for the problem of world hunger.

7. Work on a special project in the church and/or community that would be a Christian response to the problem of world hunger.

C. MATERIALS NEEDED

The following items will be used in one or more of the three sessions.

Food, Bibles, paper, pencils, slides, poetry forms, creative activity materials.

D. SEQUENCE OF SESSIONS AND ACTIVITIES

FIRST SESSION. . . .SHARING MEALS WITH OTHERS

FIRST ACTIVITY — FAMILY MEALS

Persons can meet in family groups. Each parent and each child will share some of their own memories and feelings. If there are some in the total group who are not with their families then they can join with one of the family groups. Or, if the total group is composed of a mixture of persons without reference to family structure then the group can be subdivided in any one of several ways in order to have small groups of four to five persons.

Parents, or adults, share first. Briefly describe from memories of childhood one or two experiences of meals shared with the family.

Children share after the adults. Describe one or two things they like about sharing meals with their families.

Or, another way for younger and older persons to share with each other is to describe the family dinner table at the time when they were young children.

> What room was it in?
>
> How many were gathered around the table?
>
> What special memories associated with the table?

SECOND ACTIVITY — VALUES ASSOCIATED WITH MEALS

Persons in the group can discuss together in two's and three's the following rank orders. There are three rank orders. Use one or more of them, or the leader can devise different ones. Be sure to give each item its own ranking. Top ranking would be "1", next would "2", and so on to the lowest. After doing the ranking, persons share with each other in the small groups their reasons for ranking the items high and low.

Rank Order #1

To eat in a restaurant would you prefer:

_____ McDonald's

_____ The Pizza Place

_____ A Steak House

_____ A Fancy Restaurant

Rank Order #2

To celebrate your birthday would you prefer a meal

_____ With one special person

_____ With your whole family

_____ With a large group of friends

_____ With a small group of friends

Rank Order #3

Which do you like best:

_____ A progressive dinner

_____ A potluck supper

_____ A picnic

_____ Dinner in a restaurant

THIRD ACTIVITY — PREPARING A MEAL

The transition from ranking to preparing a meal needs to be managed by the leader by talking about the connection between the values we have regarding meals and actually planning a meal that will be shared together.

If the meal can be shared immediately after the planning then some preparation needs to be made ahead of time for persons to bring food or for food to be available. On the other hand, if the meal will be later it should happen sometime during the week before the next session.

There are many elements that could be planned for, depending upon the number and ages of persons and the time available. Some possibilities include:

Salads	Table decorations
Beverages	Name tags
Main dishes	Placemats
Desserts	Songs for fun and inspiration
Room arrangement	Prayer or singing grace before meal

Interaction around the tables and other ideas you may have

Persons can volunteer for various responsibilities and then work with others to make the necessary plans for the meal.

FOURTH ACTIVITY — SHARING THE MEAL

SECOND SESSION. . . .MEALS WITH JESUS

FIRST ACTIVITY — SETTING THE STAGE

The last time we were together we shared a meal. We have considered the importance of meals in our lives and especially the importance of relationships with others with whom we share meals. Today we are going to focus on some meals that persons shared with Jesus as described in the gospels.

We are going to work in groups of two or three.
        (allow time for the groups to get organized)

Together select one of the following meals to think about:

1. Dinner in Matthew's house . . . . Matthew 9:9-13
2. Feeding of the 5000 . . . . John 6:1-15
3. Meal at house of Simon the Pharisee . . . . Luke 7:36-50
4. The Last Supper . . . . Luke 22:14-20
5. Washing the disciples' feet . . . . John 13:2-20

SECOND ACTIVITY — DISCUSSING A MEAL WITH JESUS

In the groups of two or three look at the account of the meal in the scripture and find answers to three questions:

> *1. What do you think was the reason for the meal?*
>
> *2. Who were the participants in the meal? Why do you think they were present?*
>
> *3. What were Jesus' words and actions?*

If there are non-readers then a reader could read aloud the passage and the questions and together come up with some answers.

Persons from one group join with another group focused on the same meal. In this larger group discuss two more questions. These questions do not have specific, right answers, but persons can express their own ideas and feelings.

> *1. What do you think Jesus was trying to communicate through his actions and words at the meal?*
>
> *2. If you could have been a participant at the meal what are some thoughts or feelings you might have had?*

THIRD ACTIVITY — COMPARING THE MEALS

The whole group will now be restructured into groups of five persons. Each person represents a different one of the five meals that were studied. There will most likely not be an equal distribution of persons and meals so if there are two persons representing one meal, that is okay. Also, if one of the meals is not represented in a group, that is okay.

In groups of five, representing various meals, persons can discuss one or the other of two questions. Persons are to respond to the questions in the first-person as if they had been one of the participants in the meal. This is a little like role playing and helps persons really identify with the subject of their study.

   1. What was your impression of Jesus as a result of sharing the meal with him?

   2. What did you learn about yourself through this encounter with Jesus at the meal?

FOURTH ACTIVITY — CREATIVITY AND CELEBRATION

Respond to the study and role play of the meals with Jesus by spending some time creating some visuals, poems, litanies or other resources that would be used as a part of a brief celebration.

1. Illustrate the song "LET US BREAK BREAD TOGETHER" with slides.

   Each could focus on one line of the song creating one or two slides. (see pages 55 & 56 for instructions regarding slide making)

2. Use poetry forms to create some poems that emphasize meals with Jesus. (see page 75 for sample poetry forms)

3. Prepare a litany with a series of affirmations and a corporate response that summarizes some of the ideas and feelings connected to meals with Jesus.

4. Some simple food could be available and a small group could prepare it to share with the group. The food could include:

bread	dates	raisins	grape juice	grapes
figs	melon	bananas	nuts	

The time of celebration for the closing could follow an order such as:

   Share poems

   Litany

   Share food

   Sing song, LET US BREAK BREAD TOGETHER, and show slides

THIRD SESSION. . . .SACRAMENT OF HOLY COMMUNION

Churches and groups or persons from many liturgical traditions will be using these session plans. Therefore, we do not intend to present a particular theology of the Sacraments, but rather to provide an outline of a process that will enable leaders to present whatever theology is appropriate to the particular church.

Even if the younger persons in your intergenerational group are not able to participate in the Sacrament of Holy Communion they are probably interested and/or curious about what happens and what the symbols and actions mean.

FIRST ACTIVITY — REVIEW THE ACCOUNT OF THE LAST SUPPER

The persons who focused on the Luke passage of the Last Supper in the previous session could lead the whole group in a review of that event. The questions that were explored last week will provide a good outline for the review.

   1. What was the reason for the meal?

2. *Who were the participants?*

3. *What were Jesus' words and actions?*

4. *What do you think Jesus was trying to communicate through his actions and words?*

5. *If you could have been a participant at the meal what are some thoughts or feelings you might have had?*

The leader could provide some help by conducting more of an interview rather than having the persons make a report.

SECOND ACTIVITY — CELEBRATING THE LORD'S SUPPER IN OUR CHURCH

The intent of this activity is to acquaint everyone with the way Communion is celebrated in their church. These are two possibilities:

A. Invite the minister or priest to attend the class session and at this point he could share with the group the what, why, and how of Holy Communion in this church.

B. If time and circumstances permit, it would be a good experience for the group to meet with the minister or priest at the communion table or alter in the sancturay. The minister or priest could show some of the articles used in communion and explain the actions and words of the liturgy.

During this part of the session the leader or some other person(s) could represent the group by asking questions for the minister or priest to respond to. This would be like conducting an interview.

THIRD ACTIVITY — ADDITIONAL INFORMATION

This activity is optional depending on the amount of time spent and information given during the previous activity. It may be helpful to have available a variety of resources which could be used by the participants to explore further the sacrament of Holy Communion. A filmstrip, a short 16mm film, some books with children's stories, some other resource books and an informed resource person would all be appropriate, possible resources.

FOURTH ACTIVITY — RESPONDING CREATIVELY

There are several possible ways persons could respond creatively to their learning about the sacrament of Holy Communion:

a. Make a set of slides or posters that present some of the symbols associated with the Sacrament.

b. Create one or more banners that could be used as part of a processional and to display in the church during a celebration of the Sacrament.

c. If it is possible to have a communion service with the whole group of generations learning together then it may be a good experience for a small group to work with the minister or priest to plan for that experience.

d. Some children, youth, and adults in the group may have an interest and talent in music where in a small group they could write a brief song. Or, they could practice together the singing or playing of a song appropriate for Holy Communion that could be shared with the congregation.

e. Another group may find satisfaction in baking bread together. This bread could be part of a meal with the group or perhaps even used as a part of the celebration of Holy Communion.

FOURTH SESSION. . . . .SHARING BREAD WITH THE HUNGRY

INTRODUCTION

This whole session will be just an introduction to the problem of world hunger. It may be that the planning group will want to proceed to another Unit of three to six sessions which will focus on more of the examples of, causes of, responses to, and solutions to the present and future crisis of world hunger.

One of the best units of study we have previewed is:

A WORLD HUNGRY produced by Franciscan Communication Center
1229 South Santee Street, Los Angeles CA 90015

This is a set of five filmstrips: "You May Have Heard", "How Hunger Happens", "The Green Counter-Revolution", "Knowledge and Lifestyle", and "Church and Political Action". The filmstrips may be purchased from the producers or borrowed or rented from a Catholic Diocesan Resource Center or other source.

The filmstrip guides suggest ways to include the showing of the filmstrips as a part of a larger program.

Also available from Franciscan Communication Center as part of the program A WORLD HUNGRY is a family activities booklet, "The Empty Place". This booklet offers many, many very practical suggestions for families to help them become more aware and responsible regarding world hunger.

FIRST ACTIVITY - WHEN HAVE YOU BEEN HUNGRY?

Persons could talk together in small groups responding to one or more of the following questions:

What are some times when you have been hungry?

What feelings or thoughts have you had when you were hungry?

What are some ways that your experiences of hunger are similar or different to the experiences of persons who are hungry every day of their lives?

Describe some things you know about the problem of world hunger.

SECOND ACTIVITY - GETTING THE FACTS

If there is a hunger task force in the church or in the community it is possible that they already · have done some research and have a lot of facts about the problems of hunger in your own community, state, nation and the world.

There are several ways that this information could be presented.

a. Several informed resource persons could meet with small groups of various ages or interests to explore some of the facts of the problem.

b. Interest centers could be arranged for persons in the group to focus on one center or circulate among several centers.

c. A representative from an organization such as C.R.O.P. Heifer Projects, Inc., Bread for the World, Church World Service, or Catholic Relief Services could be invited to visit the group to share information, a film, and suggestions of what the group and the church can do to respond to the problem of world hunger.

THIRD ACTIVITY - DECIDING TO ACT

The leader can guide the group in a process of brainstorming possible actions, categorizing actions, and selecting specific actions.

Involve the whole group together, or in small groups, in a process of brainstorming all the possible actions the individuals in the group and the group itself could do to respond to hungry persons.

Every suggestion is okay. Write all the suggestions down on newsprint or overhead transparency so that they will be visible to the group. Look at the total list and put them in several categories. Identify the categories by a descriptive title.

Select the top ten actions that seem to be most possible and most effective in relation to the group and the church.

Everyone can rank the top ten actions in order of priority from most effective and possible to least effective and possible.

When the group has identified two or three top priority actions that most persons can agree to then perhaps a task group should be formed to develop a strategy in order to help the group implement its top-priority actions.

FIFTH ACTIVITY — CONCLUDING DISCUSSION AND PRAYER

A discussion to conclude the session could be focused on a question such as:

> In the Gospel of John (6:35) Jesus said, "I am the bread of life, he who comes to me will never be hungry." What are some ways to interpret that saying of Jesus in light of our experiences in the last several weeks and especially this week?

It is not intended that the discussion be long and involved but rather just a way of summarizing the focus on meals and hunger.

The session could be ended with a prayer or litany in which members of the group are encouraged to participate by expressing their own thoughts, feelings and concerns.

A Note to the Leader

As the leader begins planning for this unit it would be wise to ask the following questions:

> What experience of the world do the students have?

> What understanding or experiences do the students have of hunger?

> Are there concrete experiences that can be provided in class to bring the concepts of WORLD and HUNGER alive?

Most children do not begin to have a "world view" until 5th or 6th grade. Even though TV has made children more aware of a larger world and more familiar with names of countries they still find it difficult to comprehend distance or understand geography. Their world is still very much centered in the family, church, and community where they live. The leader of this unit would be wise to be sensitive to the conceptual development of the children in the group. Checking out the school to see what concepts the children have of the WORLD at various age levels would be a very smart move.

As we looked over what we had written for this unit we noticed that there was a heavy emphasis on discussion and sharing of ideas. In order to have a discussion persons have to have information to share or experiences to share. If children are to be able to enter into discussions they must be provided the opportunities in class to gather that information and to have experiences. This is especially important in this unit because children may not have had experiences outside of class to gather information. Our hope is that the leader will plan a wide variety of activities that will involve all students in the gathering of information that they in turn can share and that will stimulate thinking and action.

UNIT SEVEN. . . .CELEBRATING ADVENT AND CHRISTMAS

A. INTRODUCTION

Advent and Christmas provide a natural time for involving families and/or persons from several generations in common learning and celebrating experiences. Many churches have planned for special activities during this season which include:

- A special intergenerational class for four weeks.

- An all day Advent Workshop for the whole church family.

- One or more Family Night Fellowship gatherings at the church.

- Four Sunday night church family celebrations.

One or more of the outlines of activities in this unit could provide the basis for planning a special intergenerational experience. In addition to these suggestions you will find a variety of other activities presented in our book TEACHING AND CELEBRATING ADVENT-CHRISTMAS. The book includes chapters on:

"Celebrating Advent in the Family"

"Celebrating Advent in the Classroom"

"Four Sundays in Advent - A Family Liturgy"

"Deck the Halls (Craft Activities)"

Plus five other chapters and a bibliography.

With the materials in this unit and our Advent-Christmas book you should be able to find an abundance of ideas to stimulate your creativity and planning.

B. UNIT OBJECTIVES

As a result of participating in the activities included in this unit persons will be enabled to:

1. State in their own words something about the importance of gifts and giving.

2. Distinguish between tangible and intangible gifts.

3. Identify some family, church, and cultural traditions related to Advent and Christmas.

4. Define in their own words the meaning and importance of the concept Messiah for Jesus' day **and** our day.

5. Express in creative ways their interpretations of gifts, giving, traditions, messiah, and the story of Jesus' birth.

C. MATERIALS NEEDED

The following materials will be needed for the whole unit. In addition there will be other, special materials needed for each session which will be described in connection with the outline of each session.

Bibles (various translations, including especially GOOD NEWS FOR MODERN MAN)

Paper, pencils,

Reference books, story books, hymnals

Record player, filmstrip projector, movie projector, screen

Newsprint and felt markers.

D. SEQUENCE OF SESSIONS AND ACTIVITIES

FIRST SESSION. . . .ADVENT TRADITIONS
OBJECTIVES
At the end of the session persons should be able to:

1. Explain several symbols that relate to Advent

2. Identify some important family, church, and/or cultural traditions.

3. State in their own words the meaning of Advent as a Season of the Christian Year.

MATERIALS NEEDED
Materials for making advent wreaths and banners

ACTIVITY ONE. . . .WHAT DOES THE WORD "TRADITION" MEAN?

The leader can guide the group in a brief introduction and discussion of the concept of tradition.

What do you think of when you hear the word tradition?

What are some examples of traditions?

Why do you think traditions are important?

What are some traditions your family has in the way you celebrate birthdays?

ACTIVITY TWO. . . .FAMILY TRADITIONS

In family groups have each member of the family tell one or more traditions that are related to the ways the family prepares for and celebrates Christmas. If there are single persons in the group, younger or older, have all those persons meet together in one group to discuss together traditions they remember in their families.

Each family or small group selects one or two special traditions they would like to share with the whole group.

Be sure to allow enough time for each family or small group to share their tradition with the larger group.

ACTIVITY THREE. . . .THE TRADITION OF ADVENT

The leader can take a few minutes to make a brief presentation that will summarize some of the origins, symbols, and traditions associated with Advent. The presentation will be more effective if the leader can prepare ahead of time some visuals in the form of charts, key words, posters, symbols associated with Advent, etc. An excellent resource for gaining some background information on the days and seasons of the Church Year is: THE YEAR OF THE LORD written by Theodore Kleinhams and published by Concordia Publishing House. This book could be ordered through your local bookstore.

The conclusion of the presentation should focus on the symbol and traditions represented by the Advent Wreath. If some families are already familiar with Advent celebrations and use the Advent Wreath in their family then they could be encouraged to share some of their own experiences.

ACTIVITY FOUR. . . .*MAKE ADVENT WREATHS and/or BANNERS*

There should be enough materials provided for each family to make its own Advent Wreath.

- cardboard or styrofoam circle for base of the wreath

- cut greens to form the wreath

- fine wire or black thread to attach greens to base

- four purple candles and a larger white candle as the Christ Candle to be lit on Christmas Eve.

All or some members of each family or household group could work together creating an Advent Wreath or a hanging wreath for the fireplace or front door.

Families who have already made their wreaths, or choose not to make one, and other persons could work to create individual or family Advent banners. The banners could be made from burlap and pieces of colorful felt. The designs of the banners could include symbols, words, shapes and colors. Banners could be small or large to be hung in a prominent place in the home or in the church.

ACTIVITY FIVE. . . .*FIRST SUNDAY IN ADVENT CELEBRATION*

The leader and/or other members of the group could prepare a brief celebration for this first Sunday in Advent. The celebration might include:

- An opening statement and lighting the first candle

- An Advent hymn or carol

- Reading from the Bible

- A Prayer

- Another Advent Hymn or carol

- A closing litany composed of statements by the participants completing the phrase "Advent is. . . ." Response could be: "O Lord, we pray for your coming into our lives."

SECOND SESSION. . . .HYMNS AND CAROLS

OBJECTIVES:

At the end of the session persons should be able to:

1. Explain the origins of at least one hymn or carol and explain the meaning of the words of one verse.

2. Connect words from a hymn or carol to words of Scripture.

3. Express in a creative way an interpretation of one hymn or carol.

MATERIALS NEEDED

Hymnals, Bibles, phonograph records of Christmas carols and hymns, and creative activity materials. Secure from city library, church library, and pastor's library resource books that provide background information on Christmas carols.

ACTIVITY ONE....SINGING

This first activity can be experienced in one of several ways:

1. If possible, the whole group could gather around the organ in the sanctuary with the church organist accompanying the group in their singing of favorite Christmas carols and hymns.

2. Everyone who plays an instrument could practice several selected carols during the week then for this session could accompany the others in their singing.

3. One or more phonograph records of Christmas music could be used to guide the group in their singing.

The time for singing is intended to help the group focus on some of their favorite hymns and carols. The singing is for enjoyment. Spend about 15 minutes on this activity.

ACTIVITY TWO....SELECT A CAROL TO STUDY

Each person or family selects one favorite Christmas carol or hymn to be the focus for the rest of the session. The carols can be selected from a list prepared by the leader or from the church hymnal or some other source.

If two or more persons select the same carol then they could work together as a small group if they choose.

Instructions should be printed on a poster or some other visible format so that persons can work at their own pace. The instructions could be as follows:

> NOTE: *For persons, especially non-readers, who are not able or interested to do the research there could be a story table, a listening center, or some other similar activity that they would enjoy.*

**Instructions For Thinking
About Christmas Carols.**

Step 1   Select a favorite Christmas carol to be the focus of your thinking for the rest of the session.

Step 2   Check to see if anyone else selected the same carol. You can work together if you choose to.

Step 3   Look in the resource books to see if you can find answers to some of these questions:

> *Who wrote the words and music?*
>
> *When and where was the carol written?*
>
> *What are some interesting facts related to the circumstances which produced this carol?*
>
> *What do you think is the primary message of this carol?*

Step 4   Use your Bibles and other resource books to find at least one passage of scripture that relates to the same theme as the first verse of the carol.

Step 5   Use overhead transparencies, write-on slides, or poster boards to create a visual expression of what you feel is the message of the carol.

The carols, scriptures, and visual expressions will be shared with the whole group.

ACTIVITY THREE. . . .SHARING CHRISTMAS CAROLS

Each person or group can share what they have discovered and created in response to their involvement with a carol. The procedure could be:

1. Share some interesting information

2. Read a passage of scripture

3. Project or show the visual expression while the whole group sings the first verse of the carol.

The singing and the session could be concluded with a brief prayer or litany.

FOLLOW-UP ACTIVITY

After spending time getting familiar with several Christmas carols it is possible the group could share their experience with others in one of the following ways:

1. As a part of a family Christmas Eve service

2. By presenting a brief program in a Convalescent Hospital.

3. With another class in the church.

4. In the regular church worship service.

THIRD SESSION. . . .FOCUS ON GIFTS AND GIVING
OBJECTIVES:

At the end of this session persons should be able to:

1. Distinguish between tangible (material) and intangible (relational) gifts.

2. Suggest some gifts they would like to give to others.

3. Illustrate in a creative way the meaning of a passage of scripture focused on giving.

MATERIALS NEEDED

The book and/or filmstrip THE GIVING TREE. Book by Shel Silverstein, Harper and Row, Publishers. Filmstrip is a Stephen Bosustow Production.
Creative activity materials
3x5 cards for identifying gifts.

ACTIVITY ONE. . . .DISCUSS SPECIAL GIFTS

Persons in the group are divided into small conversation groups of three or four persons. Each person is to think about and share with others in the small group his/her thoughts on one or more of the following questions:

What is a special or favorite gift you have received?

When were you really surprised by a gift?

What is a special gift you have given to someone?

There does not need to be sharing with the larger group. The conversation in the smaller groups is sufficient by itself.

ACTIVITY TWO. . . .BRAINSTORMING ABOUT GIFTS

Each person first write down as many words that come to mind that are associated with the concepts of gifts and giving. Allow no more than two minutes.

Each person is to select three most important words to express the meaning of gifts or giving.

On a sheet of newsprint, or perhaps overhead projector, write out a composite list of words. Try to collect thirty or more words.

The transition from our words about gifts to scripture passages focused on gifts is important. Now that we have identified some of our words related to gifts let's see what some writers in the Bible had to say about the same subject.

ACTIVITY THREE. . . .BIBLE PASSAGES FOCUSED ON GIFTS

There are two ways to approach this activity:

a. Offer a list of preselected passages from which persons or groups can choose.

b. Provide resources such as Concordances, Dictionaries, Word Books, and Index in GOOD NEWS FOR MODERN MAN for persons and groups to search for their own passages.

It is possible to offer both alternatives to the same group so that they will not only have the choice of which scripture passage from a list, but also the choice to search for their own passage.

Some scripture passages to include could be:

a.	Matthew 6:1-4	Teaching about charity
b.	Matthew 7:7-12	Ask, Seek, Knock
c.	Matthew 25:35-40	In as much as you did it for the least. . . .
d.	Mark 12:41-44	The Widow's offering
e.	Mark 14:3-9	Jesus anointed at Bethany
f.	Luke 10:5-37	Parable of the Good Samaritan
g.	Luke 15:11-32	Parable of the Loving Father
h.	John 3:1-21	Jesus and Nicodemus

After selecting a passage to focus on, persons in small groups can discuss the following questions:

What does this passage tell us about giving?

What are some feelings that can be associated with this passage?

What are some connections between the passage and our own ideas and feelings about gifts, giving and receiving?

When the small groups have had enough time (5-10 minutes) to discuss the questions, the leader can bring the whole group back together and provide some time to share what insights they have gained. The leader will need to ask some probing questions to stimulate and guide the discussion.

NOTE TO PLANNERS. . . .Consider the following alternatives. . . .

If you have enough time and you judge that your group is capable of the following activity, you will find that they will be helped to become more specific and concrete with the intangible (relational) aspects of giving. It is possible that this could be the last activity in the session, or it could lead to an activity of creative expression.

Another alternative would be to go directly to the presentation of the story THE GIVING TREE to be followed by discussion and time for creative expression.

Or, all the activities could be done in the sequence as presented in this outline.

ACTIVITY FOUR. . . .PRACTICE GIFT GIVING

Prior to the session, the leader needs to prepare a set of 3x5 cards with open ended statements on them. Each card would have a different statement such as:

"Listening feels like a gift when. . . ."

"Caring feels like a gift when. . . ."

"Forgiveness feels like a gift when. . . ."

Some other key words that could be used, followed by the phrase,
"_____ feels like a gift when. . . ."

- Helping	- Sharing	- A meal
- A phone call	- Friendship	- A friend
- A visit	- A letter	- Acceptance
- Flowers	- A compliment	- Add your own.
- An invitation	- A photograph	

Persons are asked to choose a card and to think of a personal experience or to imagine a possible experience that could be used to help complete the statement. For example: "A letter feels like a gift when I open my suitcase and find a letter Pat has written and hidden in my shirts." What we want to try to accomplish is for persons to be as specific and concrete as possible in identifying some gifts that are more intangible than a pretty, wrapped package.

After completing the statement on the card the next step is to share the statement with a friend or someone in the family. In pairs persons can share some of their feelings about the "gift".

Another possible step is for each person to search in the group for another person who can identify with the "gift" that was described on the card.

Still another alternative is for each person to write a "gift message" that could be given to someone else in the group.

ACTIVITY FIVE. . . .THE GIVING TREE

Tell or read the story THE GIVING TREE. (Pat has told the story accompanied by a flannel-board) or, if you can obtain the filmstrip with the same words and visuals as the book it would be very effective to present the filmstrip. (See page 140 for name of producer).

One basic question could be asked to begin a brief discussion to reflect on the story and the other experiences in the session.

> *What are some connections you would make between this story and the Bible passage and personal experiences we have shared?*

ACTIVITY SIX. . . .CREATIVE EXPRESSION

Persons can choose one of the following ways to express creatively some of their own insights or feelings regarding **gifts.**

1. Write a poem. Use free verse or possibly one of the poetry forms available.

2. Select one or more photographs from the PICK-A-PICTURE BOX **and** write a brief statement or story about the photographs that says something important to you about gifts.

3. Use some available puppets to make up a story, or puppet play, that will say something about gifts.

4. Draw a picture (on transparency, paper, or poster board) that illustrates something important about gifts.

5. Make a message poster (or banner) to communicate a brief message about gifts.

When everyone is finished with his/her creative expression, time could be taken to share with one another as the closing activity.

FOURTH SESSION. . . .THE BIRTH OF JESUS

OBJECTIVE

At the end of the session persons should be able to:

a. Interpret the meaning of the story of the birth of Jesus in a verbal or visual way.

MATERIALS NEEDED:

A variety of books and stories of Jesus' birth, resource books, a collection of teaching pictures or art prints.

INTRODUCTION

This session is designed to employ four different learning centers. Persons can choose whichever center interests them. Each center requires a different level of reading and analysing skills so that leaders should be especially aware of younger readers to be sure they don't end up in the center requiring the greatest skill. The outline under each center is written as if the instructions are being read by the participant.

> *NOTE: It is possible that the leaders could choose the activities outlined for one center and plan to guide the whole group through those activities. If this is done then the whole unit could be expanded by one or two additional sessions.*

1. THE MESSIAH

A. **Read** the following statement about the concept of Messiah.

In the time before Jesus, the Jews were expecting a Messiah to come to save them. The Jews had several images of what their Messiah would be. For some persons Jesus was identified as the Messiah they were expecting; for others he was the opposite of what they were expecting.

B. **Write** down a list of four or more questions that come to mind after reading the above statement. What are some questions that would guide your further study of the concept MESSIAH?

C. **Use** the resource books and **search** for answers to some of your questions.

D. **Check** some or all of the following passages that focus on the Jews expectation of a Messiah.

Isaiah 9:2-7, 40:1-11, and 52:13-53:6
Amos 9:11-15   Jeremiah 31:31-34   Micah 5:2-4   Malachi 3:1-5

E. **Work** on **one** of the following activities:

1. Write your own interpretation of how you see Jesus as a Messiah who fulfilled the expectations of persons in history.

2. Write a letter to a friend telling about why our world needs a Messiah today and how Jesus is that Messiah.

3. Create some visual symbols that would illustrate the concepts of Messiah and Jesus.

2. COMPARING TWO STORIES OF JESUS' BIRTH

A. Below are ten questions. First, read the Matthew passage and write answers in column A. Then, read the Luke passage and write answers in Column B. Be sure to answer the questions only on the basis of what you read in each passage.

B. Answer as many questions as you can from each passage.

A MATTHEW 1:13-2:12	QUESTIONS	B LUKE 2:1-20
1.	In what city was Jesus born?	1.
2.	Where in that city was Jesus born?	2.
3.	Where did Mary and Joseph live?	3.
4.	Why did they go to Bethlehem?	4.
5.	What ruler is mentioned?	5.
6.	Is a star mentioned?	6.
7.	Are angels mentioned?	7.
8.	Who shows up in Bethlehem?	8.
9.	What do they bring?	9.
10.	What "voices" of authority are quoted?	10.

C. Look at your answers. What are some differences and similarities between the two passages? How do you account for the differences? What is the basic message that is the same in both accounts of Jesus' birth?

D. Choose one of the books or stories on the Resource Table or view one of the filmstrips that presents the birth of Jesus. After reading this account of Jesus' birth answer several questions:

Which scripture passage does this story follow?

Does this story combine the two scripture passages?

E. Work on one of the following activities:

1. Write a letter to one of the authors (Matthew, Luke, or of the other story or filmstrip) asking him questions or telling him what you think of his story about Jesus' birth.

2. Select from the collection of pictures and art prints a series of visuals that present Jesus' birth in a creative way for you. Share your visuals with someone else telling why you selected what you did.

3. Prepare a way to tell the story of Jesus' birth in your own words. You could use pictures, figurines from a nativity set, or a flannel board. Then tell the story to your own family, to some persons in the group, or in another classroom in the church.

3. WRITE A FILMSTRIP SCRIPT

A. Select one of the filmstrips that are available which present the story of Jesus' birth. (Use whatever filmstrips you have available that would be appropriate.

1. LORD COME, by John and Mary Harrell

2. MARY'S STORY, an ARCH Book filmstrip from Concordia

3. THE HOLY NIGHT, from Weston Woods

B. Review the filmstrip by looking at all the frames. You are to look at the filmstrip **without** the script.

C. Start with the first frame and write a brief (one or two sentences) script for each frame of the filmstrip.

D. After finishing the writing go back and view the filmstrip and read your script to see if there are any corrections or changes to be made.

E. It is possible to record the script by using a portable cassette recorder.

F. Now you are ready to present your script with the filmstrip to the whole group.

4. CREATE SLIDES FOR A SCRIPT

A. Select one of the scripts from the above filmstrips.

B. Read through the script so that everyone in the center becomes familiar with it.

C. Divide the frames of the script among the persons in the center so that each one will have two or more frames to work with.

D. Use Write-On Slides, scratch slides, or picture-lift slides to illustrate the script for each frame. (See page 53 for slide making directions.)

E. Put all the slides together and present the whole set of slides while reading the script that accompanies each slide.

F. Now you are ready to present your slides with the script to the whole group.

UNIT EIGHT. . . .CELEBRATING EASTER

A. INTRODUCTION

In this three session unit we intend not only to focus on Jesus' death and new life but on death and new life as part of the natural life-cycle. It is important to recognize that change is a part of living and change offers opportunities for beginnings as well as endings. Families will be helped when they can think about death, change and new life at a time other than a real-life crisis. Unfortunately most families do not find these opportunities except when there is a death in the family or community and everyone is emotionally distraught. It is our hope that this unit will help persons to think about birth, life, death, change and about Jesus' death and resurrection in order to share their growing understandings of what this all means to them personally.

When this unit was used in our church one of the objectives was for the students to create twelve banners that could be presented on Easter Sunday as a part of the Worship Service. The banners were large and beautiful. During the first hymn the students processed with the banners and placed them in stands around the walls of the Sanctuary.

The number of sessions for this unit will be determined by several factors: how many persons are involved, how much time for each session, whether the banners are small for family use or larger for display in the sanctuary, and whether or not you want to include some additional learning activities. If you plan to create large banners then one session will be needed for planning and designing the banners and another session will be needed to construct the banners.

Additional activities that could be adapted for intergenerational groups are included in our book TEACHING AND CELEBRATING LENT-EASTER. Some of these activities could be used to extend the unit or in place of the activities presented in this unit.

B. UNIT OBJECTIVES

As a result of participating in these activities included in this unit persons will be enabled to:

1. Describe the process of birth, change, death, and new life that happens in the life-cycle of living things in nature.

2. Compare changes in nature and in persons' lives to the changes that happened to Jesus.

3. State in their own words why Easter is the most significant holy day in the church year.

4. Identify several symbols of Jesus' resurrection and explain what the symbols mean.

5. Use symbols, words, colors, and shapes to create a banner.

C. MATERIALS NEEDED

The materials needed for each session are listed at the beginning of the description of each session.

D. SEQUENCE OF SESSIONS AND ACTIVITIES

FIRST SESSION. . . .JESUS DIED, BUT LIVES!

Materials needed:

Church hymnal, creative activities materials, and American Bible Society film, IT IS WRITTEN.

FIRST ACTIVITY - SINGING

Sing one or two verses from JESUS CHRIST IS RISEN TODAY. It is helpful to have the words printed out on a chart for everyone to see. If you do not have a piano or pianist perhaps the choir could record the song for you during the weekly rehearsal and you could play the tape during class for the class to sing-a-long.

Focus for a moment on the word ALLELUIA. What does it mean? How does it make you feel? Shout the word ALLELUIA!

SECOND ACTIVITY - BRAINSTORMING

Ask the participants to share all the events of Jesus' death and resurrection that they remember. Write on chalk board, newsprint, or overhead projector all the events that are mentioned. Do not try to get everything arranged in chronological order. Accept all the events that are suggested regardless of their accuracy. (They will get straightened out later.)

THIRD ACTIVITY - VIEWING A FILM

To help focus on the death and resurrection of Jesus present the film IT IS WRITTEN produced by the American Bible Society.

The film is five minutes, in color, presenting Annie Vallotton as she creates with line drawings and words a very expressive story of Jesus' death and ressurection.

The film is available for rental from Association Films or for purchase from the American Bible Society. (See page 135 for address)

Instruct persons to look for two special things while they are viewing the film.

1. Look for the **actions** of the disciples
2. Look for the **feelings** of the disciples.

FOURTH ACTIVITY - RESPONDING TO THE FILM

The film ends with the words, HE IS RISEN. Ask, "Where have you heard those words before?" Sing again the first stanza of JESUS CHRIST IS RISEN TODAY. Shout ALLELUIA!

Discuss together the **actions** and **feelings** of the disciples that were recognized while viewing the film. Also, refer to the previous list of events related to Jesus' death and resurrection. Look at the list. Circle all those that were included in the film. Add any others that were in the film but not on the list.

FIFTH ACTIVITY: EXPRESSING FEELINGS

Persons can stand and form a circle or semi-circle.

One of the leaders can guide the group's thinking and expressing of feelings while another leader serves as a recorder of their ideas. A chart on newsprint or chalkboard will be prepared with headings like those below:

Death-Crucifixion-Good Friday	New Life-Resurrection-Easter

The group will suggest words, colors, symbols, and lines to include on the chart in response to the following questions.

Exercise One: Good Friday

When you think of the scene of the three crosses on the hill and the stormy, dark sky at the time of Jesus' death what words would you use to express the feelings of the scene?

(Our group suggested: dead, sadness, fear, darkness, hate)

Make your body into a shape that expresses **your** *feelings in response to these words.* (Leader can read the words slowly with time between each word for persons to respond.)

What colors come to mind as you think about this scene?
What form of line would you draw to express these feelings?
What are some symbols that could represent this event in Jesus' life?

Exercise Two: Easter

When you think of the scene of the empty tomb and Jesus appearing to Mary what words would you use to express the feelings of the scene?

(Our group suggested: alive, joy, boldness, love, sun, hope)

Make your body into a shape that will express these feelings. (Leader repeats words slowly with time between each word for persons to respond)

What colors come to your mind?

What form of line would you draw to express these feelings?

What symbols would you use?

SIXTH ACTIVITY: CREATING WITH COLOR

Provide paints, water colors, and chalk with paper and other necessary supplies for persons to create with color and design their interpretations of crucifixion and resurrection. Persons can choose one or more of the media to use for their creativity.

Be sure there is enough time to share the creative expressions with each other.

Note to Leader: Part of the purpose of the above activities is to provide opportunity for persons to begin associating form, color, and words with crucifixion and resurrection so that when they are ready to design banners they will have a wealth of ideas. The chart that the leader made while the exercises were going on recording the responses of words, symbols, lines, colors, etc. will be a valuable reference point for students when they begin their designs for the banners.

SECOND SESSION: BIRTH, LIFE AND DEATH

Materials Needed

Filmstrip A TIME FOR EVERYTHING

Books and stories, flannelboard, paper, pencils, pictures.

Worksheets,

Seeds, glue, construction paper

Items for scavenger hunt

Young Readers Book of Christian Symbolism

FIRST ACTIVITY—GETTING STARTED

Spend a few moments singing JESUS CHRIST IS RISEN TODAY

The leader can introduce the theme for the day by calling attention to the pictures, charts, and centers that are arranged around the room. Explain briefly what is meant by the words life-cycle, emphasizing the naturalness of birth, growth, change and death.

SECOND ACTIVITY—VIEW A FILMSTRIP

Try to buy or borrow the filmstrip A TIME FOR EVERYTHING to share with the group.

> A TIME FOR EVERYTHING, color, sound, 40 frames
> Part 4 of a series "Discovering God's Creative Goodness"
> by Mary and Herb Montgomery. Available from Winston Press,
> 25 Groveland Terrace, Minneapolis, MN 55403.

The filmstrip has a very simple script and beautiful photography that presents very simply the essence of life and death from a Christian perspective.

There are several possible ways to use the filmstrip:

1. Show the filmstrip from beginning to end with the **recorded script**. Then spend some time with discussions.

2. Show the filmstrip and **read** the script. This allows time for reflection and for the leader to amplify the narration for some of the frames.

3. Present the filmstrip with recorded script, work together in an exploring activity and then view the filmstrip a second time with or without sound.

THIRD ACTIVITY—GROUP DISCUSSION

Discussion could begin by reflecting on the filmstrip with some questions such as:

How did the filmstrip make you feel?

What are some experiences you have had with death?

When you think about heaven what are some of your ideas and feelings?

What are some connections between the filmstrip and the study last week of Jesus' crucifixion and resurrection?

The leader can help build some of the bridges between last session and this session.

FOURTH ACTIVITY—RESPONDING WITH FEELINGS AND MOVEMENT

Reflect on the mystery of Jesus' resurrection. Ask the students what they think happened to Jesus' body at the time of the resurrection. What form do they think he had when he appeared after the resurrection to the disciples?

There are many things that experience change as part of their life-cycle. List several of these things. (Caterpillar, tadpole, seeds)

Focus on Caterpillar and Butterfly. Use body movement to experience this change. Lead the group to get on the floor and make their bodies look and feel like a caterpillar. The leader may say something like the following to lead the group in the experience.

You are long and fuzzy. You have crawled onto a big glossy beautiful green leaf. It smells so good you take a big bite out of it. You crawl off the leaf and onto a branch. Be careful of your balance. Feel the dampness of the wet branch? It is cool and a little slippery. It is time to start spinning your cocoon. Begin wrapping the silky thread around you. Bend your body to fit into the small space. It is getting dark. You feel alone, sleepy, and strange. You must wait a long time for the change to take place. You feel the change happening, but do not understand what is happening or what the end result will be. Then one day you realize you feel different, you want to break out of your cocoon. Break through the wall. Stretch. Try your wings. Fly! You feel free and alive.

The leader should lead the group by taking time with the fantasy. Pause between ideas so that the students have a chance to move and feel.

FIFTH ACTIVITY—WORKING IN INTEREST CENTERS

Persons can choose one or more of the following Interest Centers to work in for about 30 to 40 minutes. (If you want to add a session in the unit you can provide opportunity to work in interest centers for another whole session.)

Center 1 - Books and Stories

Gather books from the church and public libraries. Books and stories could focus on life-cycles, death, life development stages, nature, and Jesus' death and resurrection. Books should be provided for children, youth and adults.

Center 2 - Flannelboard

Pictures of seeds, branches, flowers, fruit, etc. can be available for students to make a flannelboard poster showing the life-cycle of plants. You may want another flannelboard devoted to animals and people where persons can match baby and adult animals and/or present stages of growth of animals or people.

Center 3 - Writing Center

Have available paper, pencils and about 25-40 magazine pictures or study prints.

Instructions

Choose **one** of the following activities:

a. Select a picture and write a poem using poetry forms or make up your own.

b. Select a picture and write two or three sentences about the picture.

c. Select a picture and write three questions related to the picture.

d. Select several pictures and arrange in a sequence to tell a story. Write a short story to go with the pictures.

e. Select a picture and write about what you think happened **before** and **after** this picture was taken.

Center 4 - Animals Grow - Some Even Change

Following are two examples of worksheets that would be appropriate for this center. You will want to adapt these and add some of your own.

ANIMALS GROW - SOME EVEN CHANGE

Choose some animal to show the life cycle from birth to death. Put each stage in a section of the circle.

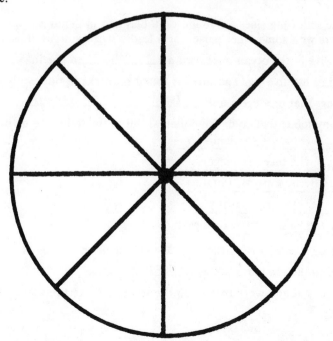

ANIMALS GROW - SOME EVEN CHANGE

What will each of the things below grow into? Put the name of each below the illustration. On the other line draw or write your answer showing what the thing will become.

_____   _____

_____   _____

_____   _____

_____   _____

Center 5 - Seeds

Seeds grow into many wonderful plants. Take a seed, glue it to a piece of paper, draw the root system this plant will have and draw the plant you think the seed will become.

Center 6 - Scavenger Hunt

Prepare a table with a wide variety of items that represent living things in some stage of the life cycle. Use the following as a sample of the list of items you could include on the table to correspond with the clues for the scavenger hunt.

SCAVENGER HUNT...FILL IN THE BLANKS

The answers to the following clues are found on tables and in pictures around the room. Check your answers with some other person or a leader when you are finished.

1. Animals that live in the ocean once used a ____(shell)____ to live in

2. A ____(starfish)____ has five legs and often is found on rocks in tide pools.

3. Find two things that produce plants ____(seeds)____ ____(bulbs)____.

4. There are many foods that come from plants. Fill in the following blanks.
   Flowers we eat ____(Broccoli, Artichokes)____
   Leaves we eat ____(Lettuce, Cabbage)____
   Roots we eat ____(Beets, Carrots, Potatoes)____
   Seeds we eat ____(Beans, Corn)____
   Fruits we eat ____(Apples, Grapes, Oranges)____

5. I grow in a tree. I carry seeds inside me. When I open up, the seeds are free to blow in the wind or drop to the ground. I am a ____(Pinecone)____

6. I live in the ground and work to mix up the soil and make tunnels for water. I am a ____(worm)____

7. I was once long and fuzzy and lived on the ground. I have lived in a dark place and have changed into a beautiful creature that can fly. I am a _____(Caterpillar)_____

8. List three animals that are hatched from eggs __(chickens)__ __(birds)__

   __(geese)__

9. A caterpillar lives in a __(cocoon)__ before it becomes a butterfly.

10. A tadpole becomes a __(frog)__

11. In the spring __(name of animal)__ are born.

12. In the summer __(food)__ grow.

13. In the fall __(corn etc.)__ ripens.

14. In the winter __(trees, animals etc.)__ rest and go to sleep.

15. I was born from an egg. I lived in a tree. I lived in the north during the summer and the south during the winter. Now I am dead. I am a __(bird)__

16. I live in a shell and eat leaves and plants in your garden. I am a __(snail)__

Note to Leader: The scavenger hunt will need to be adjusted to fit the items you are able to collect and have available in your room. A number of the questions have several possible answers. Make up your own scavenger hunt.

Center 7 - Family Conversations

All or some members of a family can work together in this center. Or, individuals from families could work together to share their memories, insights and feelings.

First, create a family tree for at least three generations. Place as many names in the blanks as you can remember. (The leader can have ditto sheets made up for students to use or can make a large piece of butcher paper mounted on the wall with diagrams for families to fill in.)

____

YOU

____   ____

Father   Mother

____ ____   ____ ____

Grandfather Grandmother   Grandfather Grandmother

Second, One parent and one child talk about birth. They may recall memories of the birth of a sister or brother, birth of a pet, stories they have heard about their own birth.

Third, Adults and children talk together about memories they have of experiences of other persons in the family related to birth, changing, and death.

Fourth, Share together some ways you have changed, others have changed, and/or some changes you can expect to experience later in life.

Center 8 - Resurrection Symbols

On Easter we celebrate the news that "Christ is Risen". Jesus, coming to life after dying on the cross is called the Resurrection. Common growing things from nature have become symbols of Christ's Resurrection. Their bright colors and beauty fill us with joy at Easter and remind us of the message "He Lives". Discover the symbols. Follow the directions on the worksheet.

WORKSHEET SYMBOLS OF RESURRECTION

A symbol is an object or sign which represents something else.

Resurrection means new life after death.

Listed below are three objects from nature which have become common symbols at Easter. Read pages 40-44 in YOUNG READERS BOOK OF CHRISTIAN SYMBOLISM* to find out why each is a symbol of resurrection. Write in your own words a sentence or two about each.

Lily   _____
              _____
              _____
              _____

Butterfly   _____
              _____
              _____

Egg   _____
              _____

---

*YOUNG READERS BOOK OF CHRISTIAN SYMBOLISM by Michael Davies, Abingdon Press

SESSION THREE - CELEBRATE THE RESURRECTION

ACTIVITY

Give each group (family groups, or groups of 5 or 6 persons) a large piece of butcher paper the size that their banner is going to be.

STEP ONE.... Decide on a theme. (What do you want to say about Easter?)

STEP TWO... Use pencils to draw the words and symbols you wish to use on the butcher paper making sure you draw them the size you want for the finished product.

STEP THREE.... When the design is complete and satisfactory to the group, decide what colors you wish to use for each part of the banner. Write the color on the drawing.

STEP FOUR.... Cut out the letters of words, and all pictures in the pieces that will be cut from felt. These butcher paper cut outs will be your pattern pieces for cutting the felt.

STEP FIVE.... Cut the felt pieces.

STEP SIX....   Use a paint brush and brush the backs of the felt pieces with white glue and place on burlap or felt backing.

STEP SEVEN....   Let the glue dry.

STEP EIGHT....   Staple top of banner to wooden cross piece.

STEP NINE....   Attach long wooden support to crosspiece.

Our banners were 3' x 6'. We used 2" x 2" pieces of wood to make our crosspiece and support. For stands to hold the banners in church we used large coffee cans filled with rocks with a 1" x 3" piece of wood placed in each can through the lid to which the standards were attached.

Illustrations:

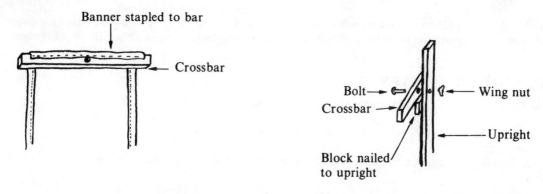

Banner stapled to bar

Crossbar

Bolt → Wing nut
Crossbar →
Block nailed to upright
Upright

View from back

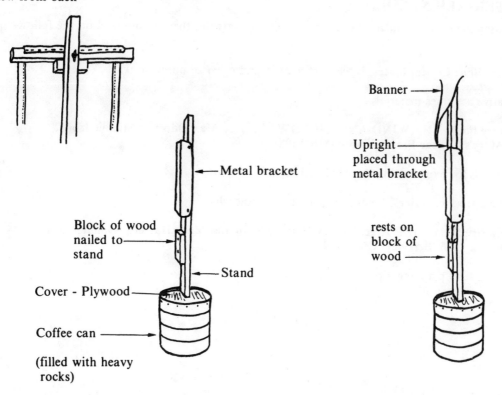

Metal bracket

Block of wood nailed to stand

Stand

Cover - Plywood

Coffee can

(filled with heavy rocks)

Banner →

Upright placed through metal bracket

rests on block of wood

UNIT NINE. . . .CELEBRATING THE GIFT OF GOD'S SPIRIT

A. INTRODUCTION

Pentecost is a day and a season that is an important part of the church year. Pentecost was a festival of the Hebrews which occurred fifty days after Passover. For Christians Pentecost is remembered as the time fifty days after Jesus' death and resurrection when Jesus' disciples were gathered together and experienced the mysterious, marvelous presence of the power of God's Spirit. In a very real sense Pentecost is the Birthday of the Church.

In what follows leaders will find a series of activities that could be used to focus on the meaning of Pentecost. The activities are not organized according to a specific number of sessions. Some churches may want to plan for three to four weeks to emphasize Pentecost and other churches may choose to have one session. If one session is planned it may be that this could be an extended session of several hours which may include a meal.

There is a sequence to the activities as they are outlined, but persons who do the planning could choose from among the activities and arrange them in whatever sequence they find appropriate.

B. UNIT OBJECTIVES

At the end of the unit participants should be able to:

1. Tell the story of Pentecost in their own words.

2. Identify and explain the meaning of the major symbols associated with Pentecost.

3. Suggest several reasons why Pentecost is celebrated in the church today.

4. Express in a creative way their own interpretation of the event and meaning of Pentecost.

C. MATERIALS NEEDED

The following items are included in one or more of the activities that are outlined on the following pages:

1. Bibles, Bible Concordances, Bible Dictionaries and other resource books.

2. Creative activities materials

3. A story book, THE WIND AND THE DWARFS by Max Odorff, available from St. Mary's College Press, Winona MN 55987.

4. Materials for experiencing the wind activities.

5. Newspapers, magazines, butcher paper, scissors and glue.

6. A filmstrip, THE FIRE AND THE WIND by John and Mary Harrell. Available from P.O. Box 9006, Berkeley, CA 94709

7. Materials for planning a party.

D. POSSIBLE ACTIVITIES

The leaders will want to determine how many sessions and the focus for each session before selecting from the following activities.

1. Focus on the concept of WIND with a discussion using questions such as:

   "What do you think of when you hear the word WIND?

   What are some experiences you have had with wind?

   What are some good things about wind? Some bad things?

   In the Old Testament the Hebrew word for "wind" is the same word as used for "Spirit". What questions does that raise or what insights come to you?

2. Persons can use Bible Concordances to search for passages in the Old and New Testaments where wind is used to represent the presence of God's spirit.

3. Bible Dictionaries and Word Books can also be used to check on interpretations, descriptions, meanings of words such as: WIND, BREATH, SPIRIT, HOLY SPIRIT, SOUL.

4. Read or tell the story THE WIND AND THE DWARFS. (see section C for author and source). Discuss the connection between this story and what was discovered about Wind and Spirit in the Bible word study.

5. Enjoy some experiences with **Wind** out of doors. Some possible activities:

   - kite flying (various sizes and shapes)

   - paper airplane flying (have a contest)

   - release balloons with messages.

   - sail paper or model boats

   - make hand held wind mills

   - blow bubbles

   - talk against the wind, close eyes, feel the wind

6. See the film DAWN FLIGHT. The film is a beautiful presentation of two glider pilots' encounters with each other. To see their artistry in flight as they capture and are captured by the wind is a sight to behold. There is a story-line that involves one pilot's struggle with and against the other. The ending is quite a surprise and leads the viewers to a meaningful discussion of self growth and understanding. DAWN FLIGHT is available for rental from Pyramid Films, P.O. Box 1048, Santa Monica, CA 90406.

7. Sing Bob Dylan's creative song BLOW'N IN THE WIND. Discuss the meaning of the words as compared with some of the other experiences with **Wind**. What is "the answer" that is blow'n in the wind?

8. Focus on feelings and relationships as expressed in key words like JOY, SORROW, FEAR, HOSTILITY, FORGIVENESS, RECONCILIATION, LOVE, COMMUNICATION and COMMUNION. Use these key words as headings on pieces of butcher paper or poster boards so that persons can select headlines, photographs and/or articles from magazines and newspapers in order to create a montage of each key word.

9. Have a discussion which focuses on the montages. Some possible questions are:

   In what ways is God's Spirit present in the experiences represented by these key words?

   What are some general impressions you receive when you look at the montages?

10. Plan a Pentecost Parade. Persons in small groups can create banners or signs to carry. Rhythm instruments or other musical instruments could be used. The parade could include singing, cheers, stunts (someone on stilts or a unicycle or other equipment), costumes or whatever else was planned. The parade could be around the neighborhood or in the church. If neighbors think you are crazy, remember that those who saw Jesus' friends on the day of the first Pentecost thought they were drunk.

11. Plan a Pentecost Festival that would be a celebration of the presence of God's creative Spirit in the midst of his people. We celebrate God's creative Spirit through our own creativity in:

writing	painting	sculpting	sewing
stitching	baking	weaving	or whatever else expresses
constructing	carving	singing	our creativity

The festival would provide an opportunity for persons to share their creativity with each other. It could include a meal (picnic) and/or the sacrament of Holy Communion.

12. Listen to the reading from scripture of the account of the Pentecost experience. The scripture reading could be responded to in a variety of ways:

- writing a contemporary paraphrase
- creating a set of slides to present the event visually
- composing a simple song
- dramatizing the event with dance, movement and non-verbal expressions without a script.

13. Reread activities 1, 2, and 3 and do something similar with the concept of FIRE.

Why do you think fire and wind are symbols that are used to represent the presence of God's Spirit?

14. View the filmstrip THE FIRE AND THE WIND by John and Mary Harrell. (see section C for address)

15. Experience a simulation activity which has as its focus the day after Pentecost.

WHAT DO WE DO NOW?*

We are followers of Jesus. Jesus has died but there have been experiences and reports of his renewed presence with some of his friends. We have waited in Jerusalem for seven weeks. Just yesterday, on the day of Pentecost, we were all together when we experienced a renewed power and life in a way we had never experienced before. God's Holy Spirit has blessed us with new excitement, energy, and hope. Today we are all together again. We are all asking ourselves and each other. "What do we do now?"

WHAT DO WE DO NOW? There are at least six possibilities. Rank the following in the order of their priority for you. (Rank your first choice No. 1 and the last choice No. 6.)

_____ I will write down some of the teachings of Jesus and important events of his life that I remember.

_____ I will speak to everyone and baptize those who believe that Jesus is the Messiah. I will go to the temple, the market place, everywhere.

_____ I will gather the disciples together. We need to organize ourselves, and to coordinate our efforts in fulfilling Jesus' instructions.

_____ I will start right away healing the sick, clothing the needy, feeding the hungry, and visiting the lonely.

_____ I will work with others of the disciples to decide on standards for our new community to determine what others must believe and do in order to belong with us.

_____ I am not ready to do anything. I will go home to think it over.

Students can be given the following instructions:

Using the worksheet that is provided, by yourself, rank the six strategies in the order that you think would have been right for the early Church. Use whatever criteria you think is appropriate.

When students have ranked the six items individually, then organize them into groups of three to five to compare their rankings and to decide on a concensus ranking for the group. If the group chooses the last one, "do nothing," then say to them, "Now that you have thought it over what will you do next?" That choice then becomes their highest.

Each group shares with the whole class the concensus of their group.

Using your highest strategy (one of the first five, not the 'do nothing' choice) spend some time looking in Acts and also the writings of Paul to find examples of ways the early Church acted out that strategy.

*Reprinted from **Translating the Good News Through Teaching Activities** by Donald L. Griggs.

129

Some follow-up activities:

A. Obtain copies of the church budget, annual report, and monthly newsletters to see to what extent each of the five strategies is reflected in those written forms. This could provide an interesting way to evaluate the Church's ministry today.

B. Encourage each group to participate in a project that would demonstrate the values of their highest ranking. For instance:

- "Write down the teachings" - students could write their own Gospel which could contain all that **they** remember about Jesus.

- "Speak to everyone" - students could decide what they want to tell others, then choose a place or group of people to go tell them about Jesus.

- "Get organized" - students could discuss together and draw up a plan of how their church ought to be organized today.

- "Help those in need" - students could identify some places in their own community where there are persons in need and plan a way to respond to at least one situation of need.

- "Decide on standards" - students could work up a list of standards of behavior and belief that should be required of everyone who wants to belong to the Church and be identified as Christian.

16. Prepare for a Birthday Party for the Church. Persons in the group will need to select which part of the party they want to be responsible for.

- Decorate a birthday cake

- Blow up balloons, make message cards, decorate balloons, play a game with them.

- Decorate the room

- Prepare refreshments

- Write a birthday prayer or litany for the church

- Choose music to listen to, songs to sing, and a simple group dance.

PART IV:
ADDITIONAL ACTIVITIES AND RESOURCES

All the ideas and plans presented in the previous Nine Units represent just the beginning of what is possible in planning for intergenerational learning activities. It is true that at the present time there is very little in the way of curriculum designed for intergenerational groups in the church, but there are many resources that can be adapted and used very effectively in that setting.

The Nine Units of session plans presented in this book are intended to be used as "planning starters." They are "starters" when they:

- **Start** your own thinking and dreaming about the possibilities of involving generations learning together.

- **Start** a program of generations learning together in your church and motivate persons to want more.

- **Start** persons to consider seriously the values of several generations experiencing the same learning activities.

If you have *started* in yourself and your church an interest in generations learning together then perhaps you will find value in considering additional resources and activities. The references listed below are all current and available as of June 1976. We have checked on them all and expect they will continue to be available for several years. In some instances there are catalogs or brochures available without cost. Write for whatever is available and gather a file of possible resources that could be used by your local planning committee.

A. A SUMMER FAMILY STYLE CHURCH SCHOOL

Fortress Press has published a very helpful manual:
SUMMER SUNDAY SCHOOL - Resource Book No. 1, edited by Gustav K. Wiencke
Available from: Fortress Press 2900 Queen Lane, Philadelphia, PA 19129

The description of the book on the cover is: "A resource book of ideas and helps to perk up a family-style church school, combining children, youth and adults."

This book is an excellent resource for planners and leaders of programs where generations will be learning together. The activities could be experienced in a variety of settings: Sunday Church School, Vacation Church School, Family Camp or Family Retreat.

Included in the book are suggestions for ten different types of programs which include:

1. Storytelling Hour
2. A Conversation Hour - Interesting People and What They Do
3. Arts and Crafts Program
4. World Missions Hours
5. Stories of Our Families
6. A People Tour of the Church
7. An Ethnic Day
8. Conversation in the Round
9. A Film Festival
10. Creativity and Imagination

B. CELEBRATING FAMILY LIFE - by Delbert and Trudy Vander Haar

In his work as Coordinator of the Office of Family Life for the Reformed Church in America Del Vander Haar has developed many valuable resources. Del and Trudy work together in leadership of Marriage Enrichment Workshops and Family Cluster Workshops.

The following resources, which were written by the Vander Haars are available from:

Office of Family Life
Reformed Church in America
Western Regional Center
Orange City, Iowa 51041

Write for information about:

- **DEVELOPING A FAMILY LIFE MINISTRY IN THE LOCAL CONGREGATION**
Thirty-nine pages of helpful information. An excellent bibliography of books, periodicals, films, and filmstrips. Outline of a strategy for developing a family life ministry.

- **CELEBRATING FAMILY LIFE**
A seventeen page outline of our Bible Study sessions that can be used in a family cluster setting. The activities in these four sessions are similar in style to the activities we have presented in Part III of this book.

- **CELEBRATING THANKSGIVING**
Two models presented that could be used by family cluster groups in a Bible Study focused on the theme and season of Thanksgiving.

- **GENERATIONS LEARNING TOGETHER IN THE CONGREGATION,**
by Trudy Vander Haar
This pamphlet describes some basic philosophy behind intergenerational education as well as provides some variety of settings and experiences where it has been meaningful to persons of all ages.

- **CELEBRATING - PEACE - LOVE - JOY** - Trudy Vander Haar
A pamphlet which contains ideas for Family Celebrations.

C. FAMILY CLUSTERING, INC.

Margaret Sawin and her colleagues have pioneered a way of structuring, leading and participating in learning experiences for family groups. They have been working at this for more than five years and have developed a series of printed resources as well as a training design to equip persons to lead Family Cluster groups.

Write to Margaret Sawin at:

Family Clusters, Inc.
P.O. Box 18074
Rochester, N.Y. 14618

Ask about the following resources:

- **EDUCATING BY FAMILY GROUPS: A New Model for Religious Education**
by Margaret Sawin. A paper on the rationale and theory of family clusters with an extensive bibliography.

- **FAMILY CLUSTER LEADER'S GUIDE** compiled by R. Gilbert and Jan Rugh.
A looseleaf handbook for leaders of family clusters with details for setting up a cluster, background papers and resource materials.

- **A RESOURCE LIST FOR FAMILY CLUSTER EDUCATION**
A listing of activities and resources helpful to leaders of family clusters. Includes stories, songs, audio-visuals, etc.

D. EXPERIENTIAL EXERCISES FOR FAMILY CLUSTERS

Many persons who have been trained by Margaret Sawin and others from Family Clusters, Inc. have begun to reproduce their own materials that they have found useful in leading family clusters. Louise Waschaw has gathered in a 32 page notebook a number of activities that have worked for her.

Write for information about the notebook, **Experiential Exercises for Family Clusters** to:

Louise Waschaw
73 Montford Avenue
Mill Valley CA 94941

Experiential Exercises for Family Clusters

- A 32 PAGE BOOKLET

- Containing 28 major activities in the areas of:

introduction
communication
self esteem
family systems
family history and identity

- Hints on songs and games

- Hints on sub-grouping

- An outline of a typical Family Cluster session

All material has been used in actual cluster settings. Designs may be adapted to fit the needs of your group. Prepared in workbook form.

Louise Waschow is a United Methodist laywoman, credentialed teacher, parent of two, and Family Cluster leader and trainer. She has been leading Family Clusters since 1973.

E. FAMILY CLUSTERING: A LOCAL CHURCH EXPERIENCE

The Rev. Alan W. Pollock is another person who has adapted Margaret Sawin's approach to intergenerational Christian Education.

Alan has written in 20 pages a very helpful, descriptive report of their experience of family clusters in the First Baptist Church of Corona. The report includes:

- a description of their program

- an outline of their goals

- session plans for eight sessions

- comments and evaluations of all eight sessions

Write to: The Rev. Alan W. Pollock
First Baptist Church
Eighth and Main Streets
Corona, CA 91720

F. MUSHROOM FAMILY

MUSHROOM FAMILY is a **family**; Fred and Margaret Lee Doscher and their child. As a family they have sought ways to involve all members of families in a creative process of growing, learning, sharing together.

MUSHROOM FAMILY is a **quarterly periodical**. Each season of the year MUSHROOM FAMILY appears with a different theme. Some recent themes were: **The Clown in Me**, permission to be real; **The World**, intimacy with our environment; **The Aging Process**, concerns with life and death, and **Childbirth**, the gift of life and its first years.

The subscription fee is $5.00 per year with special rates for multiple subscriptions to one address. Each issue offers many insights, family activities, and other resources focused on the theme.

MUSHROOM FAMILY is a helpful resource that can be used by individual families or in larger intergenerational groups.

MUSHROOM FAMILY is a creative concept and a channel of communication. Much of what Fred and Margaret offer comes from their experiences as a family and from their relationships with other families in their church, neighborhood, and a Preschool they manage called Mushroom Family Playhouse.

Write to: MUSHROOM FAMILY
P.O. Box 12572
Pittsburgh, PA 15241

Write for a sample copy of MUSHROOM FAMILY and whatever other interpretive material they have available.

G. LEARNING TOGETHER: A GUIDE FOR INTERGENERATIONAL EDUCATION IN THE CHURCH

Learning Together—A Guide for Intergenerational Education in the Church, by George E. Koehler. Discipleship Resources, The United Methodist Church, 1976.

This guidebook for planners and leaders of intergenerational education is based on the experience of scores of congregations of various denominations.

It defines a setting for IG education as "A planned opportunity for nurture, discovery, or training in which a major purpose is the interaction and mutual ministry among persons of two or more generations." The values and hazards discovered by those who have tried IG approaches are listed.

One section describes several ways of getting started, and another charts human differences across the generations and suggests ways of using these differences to advantage in intergenerational sharing.

There is a major section on planning: setting goals, choosing a model, enlisting and preparing leaders, securing resources, choosing activities, enrolling participants, and so on. And a final section summarizes eight units developed and used by creative congregations—a Sunday morning learning center, a Sunday evening Advent series, a family weekend, an open classroom, a Family Cluster program, a sixth grade class with parents, etc.

For further information contact Dr. George E. Koehler, P.O. Box 840, Nashville, TN 37202.

H. FRANCISCAN COMMUNICATIONS CENTER

Some of the most creative visual media (films, filmstrips, and slides) being produced today for religious education is coming from the folks at Franciscan Communications Center.

Write for catalogues and brochures to:

Franciscan Communications Center
1229 South Santee Street
Los Angeles, CA 90015

Their materials are available in two formats.

TeleKETICS. . . .short, open-ended, provocative films for value education and enrichment in schools, churches, and other organizations.

Multi-Media Materials. . . .contains filmstrips, slides, records, sound collages, posters, banners - combined in media kits and curriculum packages.

"These materials lead us to look INWARD for reflection and personal growth; and OUTWARD for better communication and understanding of the world around us."

See pages 89 and 93 for some specific references to films that we have used and recommended in some of the session plans.

I. AMERICAN BIBLE SOCIETY

When working with themes and passages from the Bible with intergenerational groups it is important to have printed materials that all the persons in the group can use. The American Bible Society has produced a variety of illustrated, easy-to-read, inexpensive resources for reading and study the Bible.

Write for a catalog to:

American Bible Society
P.O. Box 5656
Grand Central Station
New York, N.Y. 10017

Included in the catalog you will find some very useful materials:

- GOOD NEWS FOR NEW READERS
Thirty short pamphlets, each on a different New Testament person, event, or parable written for new readers in large print. Cost is three to five cents per selection.

- STORY—LINE FILMS
Twenty-seven 5 minute films presenting Annie Vallotton as she creates visually and verbally stories from the Bible. Each of these films could be used in an intergenerational setting.

- SCRIPTURE CARDS
Colorful 7½"x4" cards with a line drawing by Annie Vallotton on one side and the scripture text on the other. All passages are from Today's English Version.

- THE TALKING BIBLE
The complete New Testament in Today's English Version (GOOD NEWS FOR MODERN MAN) on fifteen cassette tapes for $30.75. An excellent resource for non-readers as well as others in intergenerational settings.

- OTHER RESOURCES

There are many other resources which could be used creatively and effectively with intergenerational groups that want to spend time with Biblical subjects.

Send for the American Bible Society catalog. Their resources are the best.

J. THREE MORE RESOURCES

1. **THE FAMILY CENTERED MODEL:** An option for the Church's Educational work, by William A. Dalglish.

> Available from: Board of Discipleship
> The United Methodist Church
> P.O. Box 840, Nashville Tenn. 37202

This monograph is number seven in a series dealing with education futures. In this 32 page monograph William Dalglish focuses on Fundamental Issues, Theological and Educational Assumptions, Examples of Family-Centered Religious Education, Variables in the Model, and Directions for the Future. Planners and leaders of intergenerational groups would find this a helpful resource.

2. **CELEBRATING TOGETHERNESS:** A Resource Guide for Enriching Family Relationship Through the Church by Jim and Jill Larson.

> Available from: Dept. of Christian Education
> Evangelical Covenant Church of America
> 5101 N. Francisco Avenue
> Chicago, Illinois 60625

After the pages of Introduction there are six sections which each focus on a different aspect of families being together in the life of the church.

- Enrichment for Couples

- Family Cluster Education

- Togetherness for Parents and Youth

- Parent Care Groups

- Family Camping

- Family Celebration of Worship

This brief book is not a step by step how to do it book but it is loaded with ideas and resources that could be adapted and expanded by creative planners and leaders.

3. **CELEBRATE SUMMER:** A Guidebook for Families **and**

CELEBRATE SUMMER: A Guidebook for Congregations by Elizabeth McMahon, Jeep and Gabe Huck.

> A Paulist Press Book. Available from your local religious book store or from Paulist Press, Paramus, N.J. 07652

These two books follow the same outline of seventeen topics and/or days from Memorial Day to Labor Day. There are many suggested family and congregational activities to celebrate each day, plus scripture readings, songs, prayers, and other helpful resources.

K. GRIGGS EDUCATIONAL SERVICE

Many of the resources we have produced could be used in various ways by persons who are responsible for planning intergenerational learning activities.

Write for a catalog and price-list to: GRIGGS EDUCATIONAL SERVICE
     1731 Barcelona Street
     Livermore, CA 94550

We have written several books, published by Abingdon, which can be adapted for use with intergenerational groups.

- **TEACHING AND CELEBRATING ADVENT** by Don and Pat Griggs
  This book includes 62 pages of suggestions for activities that can be planned for classes or families.

- **FOUR SUNDAYS IN ADVENT** by Don and Pat Griggs
  A collection of family activities to celebrate Advent and Christmas and a weekly family Advent Liturgy. This is a small pamphlet which is available in quantity so that churches can distribute it to families of the congregation.

- **TEACHING AND CELEBRATING LENT—EASTER** by Don and Pat Griggs
  Another resource with many suggestions of activities that can be planned for classes and families as they focus on the season of Lent and the days of Holy Week.

- **TRANSLATING THE GOOD NEWS THROUGH TEACHING ACTIVITIES** by Don Griggs
  This 104 page book contains over 100 suggestions of activities and resources that can be planned as a part of teaching the New Testament. Many of the activities can be adapted for intergenerational groups. The chapter on "Twenty Ways to Use Line Drawings" suggest a lot of possibilities for using the Line Drawings by Annie Vallotton from GOOD NEWS FOR MODERN MAN. The same activities could be applied to the use of Scripture Cards from the American Bible Society. In addition there are chapters on creative uses of slides, filmstrips, films, overhead projector and cassette recorder in teaching the New Testament.

- **CREATIVE ACTIVITIES IN CHURCH EDUCATION** by Pat Griggs
  A book with many ideas, techniques, "recipes", and suggestions for using a wide variety of creative activity materials.

L. TELLING OUR STORIES

As we plan for learning experiences in the church we find that what we are doing is TELLING OUR STORY. What follows is a brief article about telling stories. Perhaps it will help to focus on ways we as leaders can stimulate interest in the great story of God's people. Stories are a natural part of our lives. We take it for granted that we will be exposed each day to at least one story. We read the newspaper, watch television, read a book or magazine, listen to neighbors tell of recent events in their lives, tell our children about ourselves and others.

As we create events in the classroom to involve students so that they can gain new insight into what it means to be Christian, we need stories from the Bible, the bookshelf, and our own life experiences. The Bible is readily available to us, and it contains enough stories to last a lifetime. It is natural and appropriate for the teacher and the students to tell their own stories about themselves. The stories chosen from the bookshelf are often the area where teachers want help. How do you choose appropriate stories when there are so many to chose from?

Some criteria might be:

Do you like the story?

(For the story to have power to it when told, the person telling the story needs to be involved in the story and enjoy the story)

How does the story relate to the key concepts of that day's session?

(Sometimes we tell stories just for the fun of it, but if the story is to be included in the middle of a teaching strategy, it needs to be connected to that strategy through the concepts it relates)

Can you connect the story with scripture?

(Can you interpret the story theologically? If you can see in the story truths about God, and relationships between persons you can probably connect the story with scripture.)

Is the length of the story appropriate?

(Consider here not only how long the attention span of your students is, but also whether you as storyteller can remember the story in its proper order. Often the longer the story the more involved it is and the more concepts it contains. How many concepts do you want?)

Are the concepts in the story appropriate for the students who are listening?

(This question is related to the previous one on length. In an intergenerational group you may allow more concepts than you would if teaching small children. However, the more focused your concepts, the more effective your teaching.)

Does the story have descriptive words and move at a good pace?

(To hold the attention of the listener the story needs action words and descriptive words. If the writer has not included these, can you as storyteller add them without changing the story? A story draged out will also turn the listener off. Can you add descriptive words and leave out unimportant phrases to create a good pace and still maintain the essential meaning and excitement of the story? A good story captures the audience with the first two or three sentences, leads to a climax and comes to a quick ending after the climax.)

A story should be fun, capture the interest of the listener, exercise the emotions of the teller and the listener, stretch the imagination, provide the opportunity for the listener to "put on another person" to understand others better.

Curriculum assumes the telling of stories. As teachers we need to make the most of the stories we present. Teachers may want to start with a story to give a frame of reference, or build toward a story that may come at the end of the lesson. The teacher may want to follow the story by letting the students create to express what the story meant to them, or lead the students to re-tell the story in their own words through drama. The teacher can "tell" the story, present the story in a filmstrip, use a flannelgraph, use simple hand puppets, use a movie, use slides, draw on newsprint when telling the story, etc. There are many ways to tell the story and capture the listener when doing it.

Some stories we have used which represent some of the above criteria are:

(See page for one way to use the story.)	Story	Source
80	Whobody There?	Griggs Educational Service 1731 Barcelona St. Livermore, CA 94550
	Hope for the Flowers	by Trina Paulud Paulist Press New York
127	The Wind and the Dwarfs	by Max Odorff Crocus Books Terrace Heights, Winona, Minn.
	Warm Fuzzies	by Richard Lessor Argus Communications Niles, Ill.
83	Walter Fish	Alba House Communications Canfield, Ohio
91	99 and One	by Gerard A. Pottebaum Augsburg Publishing House Minneapolis, Minn.
109	The Giving Tree	by Shel Silverstein Harper and Row, Publishers, New York
91	Thank God for Circles	by Joanne Marxhausen Augsburg Publishing House Minneapolis, Minn.